INDONESIAN
CINEMA

INDONESIAN CINEMA

NATIONAL CULTURE ON SCREEN

Karl G. Heider

University of Hawaii Press

Honolulu

© 1991 University of Hawaii Press

Printed in the United States of America

91 93 94 95 96 97 5 4 3 2 1

Library of Congress Cataloging-in-Publication Data

Heider, Karl G., 1935–

Indonesian cinema : national culture on screen / Karl G. Heider.

p.   cm.

Includes bibliographical references and index.

ISBN 0-8248-1349-9 (alk. paper). — ISBN 0-8248-1367-7 (pbk. :

alk. paper)

1. Motion pictures—Indonesia.   2.   Indonesia in motion pictures.

3.   Motion pictures—Social aspects—Indonesia.   I.   Title.

PN1993.5.I84H45   1991

791.43'09598—dc20   90-25844

CIP

University of Hawaii Press books are printed

on acid-free paper and meet the guidelines

for permanence and durability of the Council

on Library Resources

this book is for
Mary Winn
John Bruton
Paul Moore

CONTENTS

Acknowledgments
ix

1 / Toward a Cultural Analysis of Film
1

2 / Cinema in Indonesia: The Industry
14

3 / Patterns of Indonesian Culture in Cinema
26

4 / Genres, Plots, and Tale Types
39

5 / Narrative Conventions
58

6 / Models for Modernization
71

7 / Moving Pictures, Moving Histories
99

8 / Constructing the Other: Folk Ethnography
108

9 / Feminism in a Male World: Contradictory Messages
116

10 / Individuals and Groups: A Matter of Emphasis
122

11 / National Cinema, National Culture
133

Bibliography
141

Index
151

Photos follow Chapter 6

ACKNOWLEDGMENTS

Because this work has engaged me for so long and has usually been a complement to other work, my debts to others are exceptionally numerous and varied. While doing other research in Indonesia funded by the National Institute of Mental Health (MH 38221) and the National Science Foundation (BNS 8310805), I began to think about films and in 1988, with the help of a sabbatical leave from the University of South Carolina and a grant from the Wenner-Gren Foundation, I was able to live in Jakarta to work specifically on cinema. I thank all these foundations and especially their review panels.

It was Gordon T. Bowles who first introduced me to the anthropological importance of popular culture in Asia. Four people were exceptionally influential in leading me to a serious consideration of cinema. Now is a chance to express my appreciation to Stanley Hoffman, Robert Gardner, Henry Breitrose, and Benjamin Dunlap. And I am tempted to mention my brother John, as well, who taught me my first lesson in the power of the cinema. It must have been around 1940, when we were both very young, and were taken to see Charlie Chaplin in *The Gold Rush*. At the appearance of the bear, John ran screaming from the theater. A second lesson, this time in the magic of the cinema, came from our father who at about the same period showed 8-mm versions of Walt Disney cartoons at our birthday parties. *Pandora's Box* run forward was fun, but when the projector was run in reverse, time turned backward and all the bad things would return to the box. Most readers will recall comparable early experiences. This book is dedicated to three who are still close to that early magic of the cinema. I hope they will come to experience also the intellectual pleasure of movies which writing this book has given their father.

I am deeply indebted to the many many people who have helped me think about Indonesian movies. Some of them are Ernest Callenbach, Carol J. Carlisle, Wimal Dissanayake, Michael Dove, Ken George, Hadipurnomo, Malie Bruton Heider, Anne and Phillip Hellman, Makmur Hendrik, Richard Howard, Eros Djarot, Teguh Karya, Umar Kayam, Kemala, Koentjaraningrat, Alex Komang, John McGlynn, the late Tuti Indra Malaon, Glen K. S.

Man, Gina Marchetti, Misbach Yusa Biran, Goenawan Moham-
mad, Ruth Berg Patterson, James L. Peacock, Ellen Rafferty,
Douglas Ramage, Abby Ruddick, Salim Said, Asrul Sani, Laurie
Sears, Krishna Sen, James T. Siegel, Ashadi Siregar, E. Gene
Smith, Saraswati Sunindyo, Dea Sudarman, Ella Syahrial, Jean
Gelman Taylor, Ted Wachter, Jan Wijaya, Putu Wijaya, John U.
Wolff, Claire Wolfowitz, Dewi Yul, the students in my Indonesian
film classes at the University of South Carolina, and an anony-
mous reader for the University of Hawaii Press. The still photo-
graphs from the Indonesian films were provided courtesy of the
Archive of the Sinematek Indonesia at the Pusat Perfilman H.
Usmar Ismail in Jakarta.

Most of them know much more about Indonesia than I shall
ever know and I apologize to any whom I have offended by errors
I may have made in my enthusiasm for Indonesian culture and
cinema.

CHAPTER I

TOWARD A CULTURAL ANALYSIS OF FILM

Movies are intricately concerned with culture. They are cultural texts, embodying within their frames the entire range of cultural behavior from artifacts to motivation. They are cultural statements, communicating messages to huge audiences. Films are cultural carriers, as well, bringing their messages to an entire nation or language area or even the world, although different audiences may read different messages from the same statement. Films in theaters, films on television, films on videocassette—all these films are sending their messages to all these voluntary audiences who watch and listen eagerly, without the inducements of heaven or promotion, without the threats of hell or prison.

The cultural implications of movies are overwhelming. The challenge to anthropology is obvious. This book develops a cultural analysis of certain films in one Southeast Asian country, Indonesia. If it were a history, then the story of Indonesian films would stand by itself. If it were a structural analysis, it could be self-contained. But it is in the nature of cultural analysis to be comparative, and so Indonesian films will be compared with American and European films. The first claim—Indonesian films are embedded in Indonesian culture—leads to the second claim: Indonesian films are to Indonesian culture as Hollywood films are to American culture. And this leads us to think not just about Indonesian films, but also a bit about Hollywood films, and to formulate some basic principles of culture, both Indonesian and American, which are relevant to their respective films.

The subject of our concern is deceptively straightforward. Films are films. Unlike many of the other bits of human behavior which anthropologists study, films offer themselves up as discrete finite

units. When I studied sexuality in New Guinea, or anger in Sumatra, the definition of the unit was always a perplexing problem
because so much of behavior is entwined with so much else. But
films are different. One walks into a bioskop in Bukittinggi, the
house lights dim, and for ninety minutes, until the house lights
come up again, one concentrates on the movie. Or one goes into a
store in Jakarta, pays money, and walks out with a videocassette
of a film contained in a small black plastic box. On my shelf here
in South Carolina I have dozens of these neatly boxed films, and I
study them. On other shelves are endless data pertaining to Dani
sexuality and to Minangkabau anger, but there is nothing as
orderly as my film shelf.

But this is an illusion. Even the approach to such nicely pack-
aged bits of culture as films involves many sorts of choices. One of
the most important concerns the ontological position of film: Is
film product or message? It is hard to say that a theory is right or
wrong. Rather, it allows certain kinds of questions which other
theories might not. Both positions will be explored in this book.
They are complementary, not mutually exclusive, yet they need to
be made quite explicit.

One can emphasize film as active agent or as passive product.
The active version takes film as communication, which opens up
questions of intentionality of the sender and awareness of the
received. There is an old Hollywood joke attributed to Sam
Goldwyn or one of the other early producers: "If you want to send
a message, go to Western Union." Underlying this scornful rejec-
tion of "message" films is the untenable notion that film is—or
can be—pure entertainment, pleasurable for the audience and
profitable for the studio, without "communicating" anything.

Communication theory in the last decades has demonstrated the
power of treating utterances as communication: What are the messages of a film, how are they encoded, what is the sender's degree
of intentionality as well as the receiver's? This approach was used
by James L. Peacock in his study of a folk theater genre, *ludruk,*
in East Java. He showed how *ludruk* plots presented models of
modern behavior which could be used by the emerging proletariat
for guidance as they moved from traditional rural settings to the
cosmopolitan cities. When Peacock's book was first published in
1968 it was a pathfinder in focusing attention on communicative
function. Ironically, more recent anthropology has backed off this

functional communication model and is now more concerned with the shape and structure of texts. Indeed in his afterword to the second edition, Peacock (1987:262) expresses some uneasiness about his youthful enthusiasms: "Were I to rewrite . . . , I would deemphasize the analysis of 'effect.' But, as noted, this emphasis, or overemphasis, did have the advantage of pushing toward analysis of the communicative event." Film, more even than live theater, is difficult to treat as communication because the utterance—the act of creation—is so separate from the reception. There is little chance for creative interaction to produce an "emergent form"—a concept which has been found extremely valuable in "live" performance of, say, folktale telling or ordinary conversation (Goodwin 1981). The closest equivalent would be, say, the audience's reaction to exciting or sad or funny moments in films. Nevertheless, we shall explore the way in which Indonesian films do send messages about modernization and gender relations.

The passive version, on the other hand, sees film as product of the culture which produced it. Movie cameras, tape recorders, editing tables, and projectors are the same around the world. But these tools are wielded by people, and the films which emerge are shaped by the ideas—the culture—of those people. As we shall see in Chapter 10, even when Indonesians do remake the American film *Blue Lagoon* it turns out Indonesian. Not just the language or the players but the most basic features of the plot have become Indonesian. It is like wax set on a surface in the heat of the sun. It remains wax, but takes its form from its surroundings. It is hardly possible even to imagine making a film outside of some culture. In reality this does not happen. And we are forced to think of culture on an unaccustomed level—of "Indonesian culture" instead of "Javanese" or "Minangkabau"—for that is the contextual level of filmmaking in Indonesia. There has never been a Minangkabau feature film.

So this second approach emphasizes films as products, as end points, and looks not for their functions but for their internal structure as it derives from Indonesian culture. That is the sense of the book's subtitle: "National Culture on Screen." There have been brilliant structural analyses of films—say, of the Cowboy Western genre (Wright 1975)—but they do not relate the genre to the culture. This is the role of anthropology. There was a brief moment in the 1940s when anthropologists made serious attempts

to move in this direction. During World War II, when Ruth Benedict tried to study Japanese culture without going to Japan, she
found that Japanese films, albeit from the 1930s, were useful
sources of cultural information. (See *The Chrysanthemum and the
Sword,* 1946.) The volume *The Study of Culture at a Distance*
(Mead and Metraux 1953) has an entire section on movie analysis
with contributions by Martha Wolfenstein, Rhoda Metraux, Jane
Belo, Geoffrey Gorer, John Hast Weakland, Margaret Mead, Vera
Schwarz (Alexandrova), and Gregory Bateson. (Half of whom, by
the way, had carried out extensive fieldwork in Indonesia before
the war.) Later John Weakland published more along these lines
(1966a, 1966b, 1971, 1972). And in 1947 Siegfried Kracauer made
a psychoanalytic study of German culture and German film, looking at how "the films of a nation reflect its mentality" (1947:5).
Martha Wolfenstein collaborated with Nathan Leites in a comparison of American, English, and French films of the late 1940s,
reported in *Movies* (1950). Their book was the culmination and,
also, the swan song of that research flurry. For decades after,
anthropologists were slow and even reluctant to look seriously at
the sorts of societies which produce movies. But this trend has
been changing recently, and along with it has come a growing
awareness of cinema as a cultural form.

As evidence of change, one can now point to Conrad Kottak's
study of television and culture in Brazil (1990), which resembles
this present book although it deals with a somewhat different
medium in a different country. Emiko Ohnuki-Tierney has used
the popular Japanese film *Tampopo* as a text to examine "the
ambivalent self of the contemporary Japanese" (1990); a panel at
the 1990 meetings of the Association for Asian Studies analyzed
an Indonesian film *(Doea Tanda Mata)* and used it as a spring-
board to discuss the cultural, political, and historical issues it
touched on; Victor Caldarola has been studying television audiences in Indonesia (1989); and anthropologists are beginning to
attend to film as cultural data even when they do not specifically
focus on it (see, for example, Beeman 1986:31–32). The University
of Wisconsin at Madison has begun a major archive of South and
Southeast Asian popular culture on videotape, including hundreds
of films from the region. Even the seminal 1950 Wolfenstein and
Leites book, *Movies,* which had been all but forgotten by anthropologists as well as film scholars, is now being thought about

again. (See, for example, Bordwell 1989:73 ff.) This present book is part of a new and renewed interest in the ties between culture and film. Thus we now consider the passive aspect of films: cinema as cultural product.

GENRE VS. AUTEUR

It will soon become apparent that not all films show their cultural roots with the same clarity. Some films are more cultural than others. The French made a useful distinction between *genre* (or formula) films and *auteur* films, which are stamped by the unique signature of the director. In American film scholarship the early infatuation with auteur theory, following Andrew Sarris (1968), has been succeeded by a great attention to genre studies (Grant 1986; Kaminsky 1985; Schatz 1988). Indeed, one can talk about a backlash against the idea that it is the director who shapes the film, and there are now voices which champion the scriptwriter or even point to various distinctive studio styles. Even David Bordwell, in his 1988 study of the Japanese auteur Yasujiro Ozu, emphasizes cultural contextualization.

Despite the arguments over auteur and genre, both are useful concepts. It is a familiar and equally important distinction in many other aesthetic areas—for example: folktales vs. novels, folksongs vs. operas, folkhouses vs. architect's creation. In talking about Indonesian musicians, Judith Becker (1979:8) has noted the same phenomenon:

> In contrast to traditional artists such as Ki Wasmodipuro and Ki Nartosabdho, there have begun to appear composers who are modern in the sense described above; men who are not constrained by the traditional system, who are not vehicles of transmission of an ancient (and ever new) tradition, but who are communicating a personal, idiosyncratic message without continuity with the past. I am thinking in particular of a musician named Frans Haryadi. He writes music for *gamelan,* but beyond using the sonorities of *gamelan* music does not relate to the vocabulary and syntax of *gamelan* music.

In cinema the differences are not so great as in these other fields. In fact there are directors who have made both genre and

auteur films. It is fruitless to attempt a precise definition of each
sort of film. But we can recognize films which are based strongly
on traditional character types behaving according to traditional
motivations in traditional plots. These are the most familiar sorts
of films. They are easy to make at a fairly acceptable level, but
their directors are not likely to be given the Oscars or the Golden
Palms—or the Citras. These are the genre films, the formula
films. The American cowboy film is the supreme example (see
Wright 1975). Ronald Reagan spent his acting career making genre
films—war, sports, and the like—and never won an Oscar for his
efforts. But the same talents which made for "merely" genre
movies were brilliantly redirected to make him president of the
United States for eight years.

The other sort of film is the result of a conscious attempt to
break out of the formula mold—to produce something different,
"meaningful," something of a personal statement. These films
may be less successful financially, but they get the prestigious
prizes. It is not surprising that Teguh Karya, deploring the way in
which the film *Terang Boelan* set the formula for subsequent Indonesian cinema (see Chapter 2), is himself a successful director and
writer of nonformulaic, auteur films which win lots of Citras.

I do not want to overstate this claim. Even the extreme auteur
film arises from a cultural context. It is hard to imagine a film of
any sort which bears no trace of its origins. But in relative terms, it
is the formulaic film which is most obviously cultural. Conrad
Kottak puts it nicely when speaking of mass culture television
products in Brazil: "They must be *preadapted* to their culture by
virtue of CULTURAL APPROPRIATENESS" (1990:43). There
is an irony in all this for an anthropologist: The most useful films
for a cultural analysis are the genre films, while the "best" films
from a cinematographic standpoint are the auteur films which
have been deliberately distanced from their cultural roots. The
most thoughtful Indonesian film intellectuals were at first puzzled
and perhaps even a bit embarrassed at my choice of films to show
American undergraduates in my Indonesian Cinema and Culture
course, or my choices of films to see in Jakarta bioskops. But a list
of the Ten Best Indonesian Films would not be the same as a list of
the Ten Most Indonesian Films. And here, as anthropologist, I am
looking for Indonesian-ness in cinema. Thus genre film.

HYPOTHESIS: INDONESIAN MOVIES ARE PROFOUNDLY INDONESIAN

This book examines Indonesian movies and Indonesian culture to show how cultural principles shape the movies and, sometimes, how the movies may influence the culture. This is as much an anthropological approach to cinema as a cinematographic approach to a culture. But first one must ask, "Why movies?"

Indonesia is so rich in traditional arts that it seems a bit odd to bother with such a recent import as cinema. Within the archipelago there is great music (the Javanese gamelan); great domestic architecture (the dramatically peaked houses of Sumatra and Sulawesi); the flourishing of practically every known sort of weaving; theater acted by humans or by puppets, the plots ranging from cosmic to domestic, the performances refined or vulgar or both. So why consider movies, surely the least Indonesian of all arts?

For one thing, many of these other forms of artistic expression had their roots elsewhere also. They were brought to Indonesia over the centuries by visitors of all sorts who came to live or trade or convert or conquer. The glory of Indonesian arts is their dynamic synthesis, which has brought together disparate elements from half a world to weave something we recognize as "truly Indonesian." The foreign elements in cinema are so overwhelming that those interested in Indonesian culture are tempted to ignore it: the technology of camera, projector, and film; the movie theater; the large hand-painted advertisements; and perhaps especially the many Chinese, Indian, and American films also shown throughout the country. All this makes it easy to reject Indonesian movies as too foreign to be of interest. We shall see how far this judgment is from the mark.

FIELDWORK IN THE DARK

My own experience with Indonesian films is worth recounting. In the mid-1980s I spent two years in West Sumatra carrying out ethnographic research on the cultural patterning of emotion among the Minangkabau. As part of a longitudinal study of how Minangkabau children learn appropriate emotional behavior, I had bought videotape equipment to record and analyze the children's daily activities. We lived in the small highland city of Bukittinggi, which by 1984 had several videocassette shops. Soon I began to rent Indonesian movies to screen in the evenings after our three children had gone to bed. I was not impressed with the movies, but I thought they would be helpful for language practice and might provide late night entertainment. Certainly I had no thoughts of taking them seriously. I had not even mentioned them in my research plans when I applied for grants.

Gradually the realization began to filter through to me that these films were not simply inept imitations of Hollywood movies. What I was learning about Indonesian culture during the day was directly applicable to understanding the films in the evening. From entertainment the films became a curiosity; from curiosity they became a challenge; from challenge they became an obsession.

In July 1984, after the first year in Bukittinggi, we returned to the United States for a year and I worked over my data, did preliminary analyses, planned for the second year, and taught an experimental course in Indonesian Culture Through Film at the University of South Carolina. I had brought back videocassettes of half a dozen films and prepared bilingual scripts for the students. By the end of that semester I had seen and studied each of the films many times. During the second year in Bukittinggi I continued the evening film viewings at home and sometimes saw films at one of the three bioskops in the city. This was good for learning something about audience makeup and audience reaction, but it had its drawbacks. Movies shown on ancient projection systems in echoing halls to noisy audiences tried my command of Indonesian beyond its limits. As a result, I did most of my viewing alone at home, and in this book I hardly touch on the fascinating topic of cinema audiences.

In 1986 we finished the second year in Bukittinggi and returned to South Carolina again. I worked up my emotional behavior data and taught the Indonesian film course two more times, getting deeper and deeper into those few films which I used for the course. By great good luck, in the spring of 1988, the third time around for the course, Ashadi Siregar paid an extended visit to South Carolina. Since he is a well-known Indonesian author, we studied a film whose script he had written, *Cintaku Di Kampus Biru* (My Love on the Blue Campus), in the course.

In the fall of 1988, during a sabbatical leave, I was able to finish the first draft of the emotion manuscript and then spend October in Jakarta. Since I am an anthropologist I suppose that this counts as fieldwork, but actually it is more like what the late Sir Edmund Leach called "yard work," or even "garden work." It was a month of cinema. I saw old films at the national Sinematek archive and new films in neighborhood theaters around Jakarta; I talked with directors, writers, actors, and actresses; I read in the Sinematek library; I attended rehearsals of Putu Wijaya's play *AIB* and Teguh Karya's film *Pacar Ketinggalan Kereta*.

For most of my professional career, films in one form or another have been a constant concern paralleling my main research and giving it important support. Making films and thinking about films gives a valuable extra perspective to the research, and certainly films offer a way of explaining a culture—a way which in some respects is more powerful than words alone. Thus, in the summer of 1960, when I was digging at the Mayan site of Tikal in Guatemala, I also made a film; during the course of my research on the Dani of Irian Jaya, Indonesia, between 1961 and 1970 I helped with Robert Gardner's film *Dead Birds* and made two films of my own; and while writing about the Dani I also wrote a book on ethnographic film. In the course of this present long-term project on emotion in Indonesia I shot extensive videotape. And I used these fiction films directly and indirectly to look at Indonesian emotional behavior. It is all these experiences which led to the central goal of this book: to situate Indonesian cinema in Indonesian culture.

I make no claims for elegant methodology in this approach. There are film studies which are based on rigorously selected samples of films (Wolfenstein and Leites 1950; Bordwell and others 1985). The hundred fifty or so Indonesian films I watched in the course of this project, however, were selected for all sorts of reasons. And the dozen films I studied most carefully were chosen early on in an attempt to cover the range of Indonesian film genres. If some seventeen hundred feature films were produced in Indonesia between 1950 and 1988 (see Misbach 1987:18), then I may have seen something like 8 percent of the total. Thus my conclusions are based on erratic viewing and uneven concentration on a few Indonesian films of the modern era (1950 to the present.)

THE REALITY OF AN "INDONESIAN CULTURE"

Not only do Indonesian films use the Indonesian language almost exclusively but, further, it is a basic thesis of this book that Indonesian films depict generalized Indonesian behavior patterns, as well, stripped of regional ethnic markers. And in doing so, these films have become an important medium for the shaping of an emergent national Indonesian culture. Throughout the book I use the term "Indonesian culture" fairly freely in a way that will perhaps jolt anthropologists and others who view Indonesia as a collection of regional cultures—see, for example, the specific rejections by Bruner (1961) and Hadipurnomo (1988) of the idea of a national culture. In fact, for decades scholars and politicians, Indonesian and foreign, have been assuming, urging, anticipating, and discussing a national Indonesian culture.

One good landmark is Edward Bruner's flat statement that "no distinctively national Indonesian culture or society has yet developed" (1961:520). Bruner's conclusion was based on his 1957–1958 research with rural and urban Batak in North Sumatra. But Margaret Kartomi refers (1979:34, n. 1) to an Indonesian government publication (Balai Pustaka [1964]) which speaks of "the uniting of the whole people in the development of a national culture." Magenda (1979) cites two Indonesian anthropologists who have discussed a national Indonesian culture: Ihromi (1973) and Koentjaraningrat (1974). As early as 1963, Hildred Geertz had identified an emerging "Indonesian metropolitan superculture" which, in a way analogous to the Indonesian language itself, was a second culture for some "bicultural" Indonesians. By the late 1980s R. William Liddle could write confidently about "the national Indonesian culture" (1988:7). Harsya Bachtiar (1985) recognized the "system budaya Indonesia" (Indonesian culture system) as one of four major competing cultural systems in Indonesia. Bachtiar was talking about a national political culture based on the constitution, laws, and the Five Principles of the Republic (the Pancasila), and he suggests that the national culture is supplanting those values and norms of the other cultural systems which are not compatible with it. But Bruner remained unconvinced: "We are deluding ourselves," he wrote, "if we believe that there is a fixed thing floating over the Archipelago labeled 'modern Indonesian culture' just waiting to be discovered and described, with the implication that it is everywhere the same 'thing,' interpreted the same way by members of the various regional cultures" (1979:300).

Actually, Indonesian films come very close to Bruner's specifications: Made in Jakarta, they are exported, in fixed form, all over the archipelago. They are "modern Indonesian culture." And our task here is to discover and describe what that means. Bruner's final phrase, though, I certainly agree with. It would be fascinating to follow one film across the archipelago, comparing the audience reactions in terms of local cultures. For of course there are regional cultures, and for most citizens of Indonesia their first language is still their regional language, not Indonesian.

In my study of emotion, for example, it was necessary and powerfully illuminating to compare Minangkabau with Central Javanese of Yogyakarta (see Heider 1991). Even when looking at the national language it is clear that there are significant differences in the way Minangkabau use it and the way Yogyakartans use it. Earlier I compared films with other Indonesian arts, but there is an important distinguishing feature. Without exception these other arts are recognizably regional and usually tied to a regional language. But as we shall see, film is not regional. It is truly national. There are no regional film industries in Indonesia. Although regional settings may be used as local color, the language of the films is always Indonesian with at most occasional local phrases thrown in. It happens that a few films violate this general principle by sharply focusing in on the special aspects of a regional culture. One of the most interesting is *Si Doel Anak Betawi* (Doel—The Betawi Kid), made by Sjumandjaja, himself a "Betawi kid" (see Ardan 1985). The movie celebrates the rowdiness of Betawians, and its title song is an almost ethnographic evocation of the Betawian ethos. But this degree of true regionalism is rare indeed.

In short, while most arts, such as Javanese batik, may be appreciated across the archipelago, they remain regional. Film, on the other hand, is made in the Indonesian language by people drawn from across the nation and is intended to be understood and appreciated by audiences in every province. This is what it means to speak of a "national cinema." And if films speak in general terms to a general audience, we are challenged to locate the pan-Indonesian cultural patterns which shape these films. And that is what this book is all about.

To some extent this problem of level complicates any use of the concept of culture. Culture is a generalization about a group of people. In ordinary talk we have no hesitation about shifting our scope depending on the context. But when we use the concept of culture in a more analytical sense, we are continually tempted to either expand or contract the scope. If we try to talk about the patterns of South Carolina culture, for example, we are urged to expand ("certainly there is not much difference between North and South Carolina") or to contract ("how can you possibly lump the South Carolina Low Country together with the Up Country?"). But this is a foolish diversion. Generalizations are always made at some specified level of inclusiveness. Different levels have different utilities. There are, of course, some obvious methodological precautions: One must not generalize at one level on the basis of data from only a small unrepresentative sample; one must specify what level is involved. But the real test of a generalization at any level is its utility for a particular purpose.

And this is the rationale for speaking of Indonesian culture in an analysis of Indonesian cinema. No one would dispute that the Indonesian language is used across the entire archipelago. An Indonesian dictionary treats the language as a single national language, even though it notes contributions from regional languages and even though everyone knows there are regional variations in the way it is spoken. Indonesian films are made in Indonesian and are shown across the archipelago. Different audiences certainly react differently in different regions of Indonesia. A violent film is probably received differently in regional settings where the cultures express and control violence differently. But it is still the same film. There is no regional tailoring in the editing of these films. (Actually, since the large film advertisements painted on canvas are locally made, one should be able to find the influence of regional cultures in that medium, but that would be another story.)

So just as we hear the national language used in these national films, we can look for a national culture expressed in these films. To be sure we can recognize sometimes Javanese or American or Indian or Dutch influences in the films. But that does not make them Javanese films or American or Indian or Dutch films which somehow speak Indonesian. They are Indonesian films. As early as 1956, Usmar Ismail declared that "the aim has been to build up the Indonesian film industry on a foundation of national cultural ideals" (1956:141).

Further, it is an axiom of anthropology that cultures change constantly. But 'for various reasons it is easy for both lay people and anthropologists to think of culture as if it were embalmed at a particular moment in time and then to ignore or deplore any changes. To recognize the changing nature of Indonesian culture leads us back to an important function of these films. They are effective vehicles for expressing the relatively new Indonesian culture. Of all the different influences on a young Indonesian, certainly some of the strongest are these films, whether seen in movie theaters or on television. We can usefully think of the national Indonesian culture as an emergent form. But cultures do not simply emerge in some mysterious fashion. There are various channels, or media, planned or unplanned, which present and shape the national culture. And few are more powerful than movies.

This book is concerned with the relationship between Indonesian culture and Indonesian cinema. It assumes that there is an Indonesian culture which is emerging and changing and, moreover, that movies are a strong force in this process.

CHAPTER 2

CINEMA IN INDONESIA: THE INDUSTRY

Before moving on to the cultural analysis which is the subject of this book, it will be useful to describe Indonesian cinema and explain how it has developed. Actually, Indonesian cinema is strikingly ahistorical. Films made before 1950 have been lost and the few films preserved from the 1950s are rarely seen. Movie theaters screen only the latest releases, and even videocassette rental shops do not carry older films. Cinema is a young person's occupation and a teenager's entertainment. There are few directors or writers over the age of fifty, so most of the current filmmakers cannot have any real memories of films made much before 1960. While Western film buffs—and especially aspiring filmmakers—can easily see and study the great films of past decades, their Indonesian counterparts will know only by hearsay even the 1950s landmarks of Usmar Ismail, Djajakusuma, and Asrul Sani. I would argue that ignorance of the past makes it harder to break away from it. In October 1988 Teguh Karya, one of the most determinedly innovative of Indonesian directors, was in the middle of rehearsals for his new film, *Pacar Ketinggalan Kereta,* when he took time out to show his cast Usmar Ismail's 1956 musical, *Tiga Dara.* The title is famous, and it has spawned many imitations over the years, but it is rarely seen by anyone. Teguh was educating his cast not to imitate *Tiga Dara* but to transcend it.

A SYNOPSIS OF INDONESIAN CINEMA

Indonesian cinema does have a history, of course, and many people have written about it. Salim Said's book, *Profile of the Indo-*

nesian Film World (1982), which has been in print through most of the 1980s, is the most accessible, but others have had their say. (See, for example, Pane 1953; Usmar Ismail 1983; Misbach 1973; Ardan 1984; Teguh Karya 1988; Sen 1988; and Misbach 1987). The fortunes of cinema have closely reflected the political situation and can logically be divided into the same periods: the Dutch colonial period to 1942; the Japanese occupation to 1945 and the struggle for independence, 1945–1949; and the years after independence, 1950 to the present, marked by the 1965–1967 transition from the Sukarno period to the present New Order of President Suharto.

The Dutch Colonial Period

Although documentary films apparently were being made and screened in the Dutch East Indies from the turn of the century, the local production of fictional feature films came relatively late. These first feature films often used traditional plots but were made mainly by Europeans or Chinese. The first production was *Loetoeng Kasaroeng,* based on a Sundanese folktale about a supernatural monkey. It was probably released in 1926—the various historical accounts often give conflicting dates. The filmography published in the special Indonesian Cinema issue of *Archipel* (1973) is a tantalizing list of titles. In 1928 the Wong Brothers released *Melatie van Java* (Jasmine of Java) and in 1930 Tan's Film made *Melatie van Agam*. (Agam is the Minangkabau district around Bukittinggi, in West Sumatra.) In 1929 Tan's Film released *Njai Dasima,* based on the legend of an Englishman, his Sundanese mistress Dasima, and their daughter Nancy (see Hellwig 1986). The next year Tan's Film made two sequels, *Njai Dasima (2)* and *Pembalasan Nancy* (Nancy's Revenge).

There is general agreement on two landmark films of the 1930s. The first, *Pareh* (1934), was a village love story (Said calls it a "film antropologis" 1982:23) made by Albert Balink, a Dutch-Indonesian journalist, and Mannus Franken, a documentary film-maker from the Netherlands. It was apparently an attempt to make a quality film, but it failed miserably in the theaters. About 1937 Balink and Franken were back with *Terang Boelan* (Moon-glow). Said says (1982:24) that it was inspired by *The Jungle Princess* (1936, with Dorothy Lamour). The scriptwriter, Saeroen, had worked in the popular theater called Opera Stambul. *Terang Boelan* was the first great Indonesian success. It brought together the famous early superstars of the Indonesian screen—Miss Roekiah, a singer, and Raden Mochtar—and it set the tone for popular Indonesian cinema which persists today. But Teguh Karya's judgment is typical: "The legacy of 'Terang Boelan' has been a stereotype film story for the industry, and an established technique which has remained undeveloped and static" (1983:10).

The Japanese Occupation

The production figures tell the story. From 1926 through 1939, feature film production in the Dutch East Indies putted along modestly at one to seven films a year. Then in 1940 it rose to four-teen and in 1941 doubled to thirty. But with World War II and the Japanese occupation of the archipelago, production dropped back to between three and five films a year.

Although the Japanese were welcomed in 1942 by many Indonesians as liberators from Dutch rule, life soon became more difficult as the Japanese exploited the labor and natural resources of the Indies to stoke their own faltering war machine (see Kahin 1952:101 ff.) The Japanese were interested in the Indonesian film industry's power to assist the war effort by making newsreels, documentaries, and even feature films. To some extent this was done. Aiko Kurasawa has cited some fifty films, at least by name, from this period, of which about a dozen are feature films (1987:102).

According to Salim Said (1982), as well as Kurasawa (1987) and Frederick (1989:109), there were several important changes under the Japanese which helped to shape the future of Indonesian cinema: Europeans and Shanghai Chinese (such as the Wong Brothers) were removed and the industry was placed in the hands of Indonesians with close Japanese supervision. The Japanese had little tolerance for romantic frivolity in film and impressed the Indonesians with the importance of using film to communicate social and political messages. Indonesians learned Japanese production styles. More attention was paid to a "proper" version of the Indonesian language spoken on screen as film became recognized as a vehicle for standardization. (This was still a period when Indonesian was being developed as a national language.)

And, perhaps most important, young Indonesian artists and writers were brought together in a central cultural organization. Out of this cauldron emerged such figures as Usmar Ismail and Djajakusuma, who were to be the leaders of Indonesian cinema after independence.

Independence to Date

Indonesian independence dates from the Proclamation of Independence made on 17 August 1945, but the next four and a half years were occupied by the turmoil of the struggle against the Dutch. Apparently no films at all were made in 1945, 1946, or 1947. But in 1948 Tan's Film and the Wong Brothers were back in business making their old-style romances again with some of the stars of the 1930s. And Usmar Ismail has credits for two films in 1949.

Independence was formalized on 27 December 1949. In 1950, the first year free of war, the Indonesian film industry went into high gear. Twenty-three films were produced that year. But only one, *Darah Dan Do'a* (Blood and Prayer), by Usmar Ismail, is preserved. It may well be that in some attic or warehouse or archive in Jakarta or Leiden there are prints of the earlier films. But *Darah Dan Do'a* is today the earliest Indonesian film which can be screened. A few more films from the 1950s by Usmar Ismail, Djajakusuma, and Asrul Sani are preserved in the national archives in Jakarta. They are occasionally shown on television or at a retrospective screening. Now, with videocassette technology widely available in Indonesia, unofficial copies of these films do exist. So videotapes may restore some of the history of Indonesian cinema.

The growing political tensions between right and left in the early 1960s led to serious divisions in the film world. LEKRA, the left-wing artistic association, and LESBUMI, its opposite number, both encouraged their people to make films and attacked the films of the opposition (Foulcher 1986; Said 1990). With the end of communist influence after the events of 30 September 1965, LEKRA disappeared along with its films. This is still an exceptionally sensitive period for Indonesians, and its effects on cinema have yet to be explored. In the aftermath of the 1965 events film production reached a nadir: There were only eight releases in 1968. Then, as the New Order government of President Suharto became established, film production rebounded and through the 1980s it stayed in the range of sixty to seventy feature films a year.

THE ROOTS AND CONTEXT OF CINEMA

From its earliest days to the present the cinema has been only one part of that incredibly vibrant, productive, and intertwined mass which is Indonesian theater. The major figures in Indonesian cinema came out of one sort of theater or another. The fact that Jakarta is so much the center of Indonesian cinema, theater, and television production, together with the economic reality that few people can live on the income from only one medium, means that today many people move easily back and forth between stage and camera. In the 1950s and 1960s many directors went to Los Angeles or Moscow for training. Now they are more likely to emerge from the Indonesian theater complex and to serve apprenticeships at home.

Of all the Indonesian theatrical genres, the most attention has been paid to the courtly *wayang* of Central Java, where people or puppets of different sorts play out hours-long dramatizations of ancient Hindu epics (see Keeler 1987). James Peacock's description of the East Javanese lower-class *ludruk* theater is an anthropological classic (1987). But there are many other genres which have been barely described in print: Randai, the folk epic drama of the Minangkabau of West Sumatra (Nor 1986); Sri Mulat, a modern Javanese comedy tradition (Siegel 1986:90 ff.); Ketoprak, the popular drama of Central Java (Hatley n.d.); not to mention modern ensembles like the Teater Populer and the Cockroach Players and even more ad hoc groups which perform both Western classic and modern Indonesian plays (Rafferty 1989, 1990). And at the more popular end of the scale, drifting about beyond the limits of theater, are traveling circuses and the *main tabus,* the fakir acts with crocodiles and tongue-piercing knives. But Indonesian movies do not even have their movie houses to themselves. Imported films, whose numbers dwindled in the later Sukarno years, now account for a majority of all films shown in Indonesia. The dominance of American, Indian, and Chinese films is to be expected. The importance of Italian films is surprising, but they may include some of the mildly pornographic films which are not even recognizably Italian.

In short, this sort of complexly interrelated theater culture is familiar elsewhere, even in America, where Hollywood and Broadway are three thousand miles apart. In one sense, then, it is an act of supreme hubris to write a book about Indonesian cinema in isolation. So be it. But let me now pay homage to the author—perhaps not yet born—who will tease out the strands linking all the different Indonesian theaters.

Production Rates

Indonesians have been producing about seventy films a year through the 1980s (see Table 1). India, at around a thousand films in sixteen languages, is by far the world leader in feature film production. The United States produces about five hundred, and Hong Kong, Taiwan, and the People's Republic of China together

Table 1. Yearly Production Figures for Indonesian Feature Films

1926	1	1942	3	1958	19	1974	84
1927	1	1943	3	1959	16	1975	39
1928	3	1944	5	1960	38	1976	58
1929	3	1945	0	1961	37	1977	124
1930	7	1946	0	1962	12	1978	80
1931	6	1947	0	1963	19	1979	54
1932	5	1948	3	1964	20	1980	68
1933	2	1949	8	1965	15	1981	71
1934	1	1950	23	1966	13	1982	52
1935	5	1951	40	1967	14	1983	74
1936	3	1952	50	1968	8	1984	78
1937	2	1953	41	1969	9	1985	62
1938	3	1954	60	1970	21	1986	66
1939	5	1955	65	1971	52	1987	54
1940	14	1956	36	1972	50	1988	64
1941	30	1957	21	1973	58	1989	101

Sources: Misbach (1987:18) and the National Film Council (Jakarta).

produce about four hundred Chinese films a year. The figures for 1985 (from Gertner 1987) are

India	912	Philippines	129
USA	452	Thailand	79
Hong Kong	105	Indonesia	63
Taiwan	183	Malaysia	10
PRC	148		

In Southeast Asia, both the Philippines and Thailand, although much smaller in population than Indonesia, produce far more films (and Malaysia far fewer). But in terms of number of films produced per capita, Indonesia is far behind even Malaysia. Here are the approximate data for 1985:

	Population in Millions	Films	Population in Millions per Film
Philippines	65	129	0.5
Thailand	55	79	0.69
Malaysia	17	10	1.7
Indonesia	185	62	2.98

Sources: Gertner (1987) and *The World Almanac.*

Audiences

Indonesian films reach their audiences in theaters, as videocassettes played at home or on intercity buses, and, occasionally, on the single government-run television channel. I was always surprised at the makeup of the audiences in the theaters—mainly teenage boys—and how scanty it was. Only toward the end of the fasting month were theaters really packed. Once, in Jakarta, my admission was refunded and the screening canceled because I was the only ticket buyer. (Admittedly, it promised to be a perfectly awful horror film.) Even in Bukittinggi, when some well-known movie stars made a free and well-advertised appearance to promote their movie (and to publicize a film they were then shooting in the province) the theater was barely one-third full.

In the neighborhood theaters in Jakarta, mothers brought their small children, apparently mainly for babysitting entertainment. But except for screenings of first-run American movies in elegant Jakarta theaters I was usually the oldest customer by a couple of decades. Thomas Doherty has pointed out that until the 1950s, film audiences in the United States were representative of the entire population—"family entertainment"—but then "the rise of television and the collapse of the old studio system destroyed that kind of universality" (1988:3) and movie audiences became mainly teenagers. Indonesian audiences may have undergone a similar transformation, although James Peacock reports the following description given to him by an East Javanese in the 1961–1962 period: "When boys are twelve to eighteen years old, they like *pentjak* (a sport mixing dance and judo). When they are eighteen to twenty-two years old, they like movies. From age twenty-two until the time they have two children, people like *ludruk*. By the time they are forty or fifty and on a pension, they prefer *wajang wong*. After they are sixty, people like *wajang kulit*" (1987:21). In any case, the current situation in both countries is the same: teenage audiences.

Few adults, at least the ones I spoke to, admit going to movies. This is consistent with one study (Subagyo 1979) which showed that the overwhelming majority of moviegoers are in the 15 to 24 age range, and almost none are over 30. Yet these same adults who do not admit to going to movies seem to know a great deal about them and about the players. Although the movie magazines and tabloids may be bought mainly by youths, the leading serious Indonesian newspaper, *Kompas,* regularly runs film notes and gossip about film stars and filmmakers, and the Citra awards at the Film Festival Indonesia commands the *Kompas* front page for several days each year.

Although there are movie theaters throughout Indonesia, the rate of attendance varies considerably from province to province. Christine Drake's (1989:88) figures for 1981 show very high attendance rates in Jakarta, Kalimantan, and Riau (in Sumatra), but very low rates in East Java and the eastern islands. She suggests that East Javanese go to *wayang* performances instead of movies. The high Jakarta figures are not surprising, but the others beg for explanation. At any rate it is clear that Indonesians are not uniformly exposed to their cinema. Drake's figures for television show much more uniform viewing across the provinces (1989:94). It is likely, as she suggests, that there are cultural explanations for these variations, but it is not clear what they might be.

The cinema can make news when a particular film deals with a historical event of importance. *Tjut Nya Dien,* a 1988 film about the heroine of the Acehnese Wars at the turn of the century, was reported on for months. Movie stars involved in scandals, of course, are fair game also. But in the intellectual press—*Kompas,* for example, or the newsweekly *Tempo*—there is serious consideration of almost every aspect of Indonesian cultural life except the cinema.

Censorship

The government film censorship board must approve the script of a film before shooting, and it must advise again during the editing stage. News items frequently appear in the press announcing titles of films which have been released by the censorship board. This is a system of prior and early constraint—much different from the way the government controls printed books. Books by Pramoedya Ananta Toer are published and sold openly for several months, for example, and then it is announced that they have been withdrawn from circulation and all copies should be handed in.

Krishna Sen (1988) has given a detailed account of how the censorship process worked in two specific cases. The Dutch film *Max Havelaar,* based on a famous 1859 novel by Multatuli, was released in the Netherlands in 1976. Although the novel is a bitter indictment of Dutch colonial policy in the East Indies and is widely available in Indonesian translation, the film aroused various objections in Indonesia and was only released by the censorship board in 1988 (and then in modified form). A second film project, this one about the Padri Wars in West Sumatra in the early nineteenth century, was never permitted to get beyond the script stage. Sen interprets the problems in both cases as violations of the principle that Indonesia must always be pictured as united vis-à-vis outside forces. This is certainly a powerful principle. But as we shall see in Chapter 10, it has occasionally been violated without censorship problems. It seems likely that the censorship board, like any other government body, is never totally consistent or efficient. But certainly Sen is correct in emphasizing the importance of self-censorship, for scripts are indeed modified in anticipation of the censorship board's review.

The forces of the marketplace have an effect on shaping films, as well. But at least in the case of scenes of sexuality and violence, the audience's demands pull filmmakers in the opposite direction from the censorship board. This is especially true of sex—an article in an imported newsmagazine (*Asia Week,* 1986) suggested that sex but not violence was being kept out of Indonesian films. The article itself was censored—painted out in black ink—in those issues sold in Indonesia.

On the whole, filmmakers are probably more clever than their censors. This, coupled with an Indonesian pattern of indirectness in expressing sensitive ideas, means that in fact many films do manage to say a lot.

FILM FESTIVAL INDONESIA AND THE CITRA AWARDS

Film Festival Indonesia is the key event of the cinema year. Its basic function is to award Citra prizes to feature films in some thirteen categories, plus another seven categories for film critics, posters, documentaries, and such. The festival is also a marketing showcase where films are elaborately screened and promoted. The festival has a political use, as well, by pressuring distributors to show more Indonesian films and fewer imported features.

The festival has varied in format, time, and location, usually moving to a different provincial capital each year. The actual ceremony is broadcast live on the national television channel and resembles America's Oscar ceremony. The recipients do not give speeches, however, and the selections are much more tightly controlled. Unlike the Oscars, which are voted on by the profession, the Citras are awarded by select committees.

Each year an annual report is published which reflects all these different aspects: pages of government documents saluting the festival, lists and photographs of the committees, lists of films, extended descriptions of the finalist films, reprints of the finalist film criticisms, informal snapshots and reports of the previous year's festival, and advertisements for films and distributors. Cer-

tainly, the festival is a major newsworthy event, and both its ceremonies and its serious seminars are well covered in the news
media.

Krishna Sen sees the festival and especially the awarding of the
Citras as the government's carrot, working with the censorship
stick, directing the shape of Indonesian cinema. Jurors often write
disgruntled insiders' versions of how decisions were reached. But a
serious analysis of Citras from year to year has yet to be made.
Certainly in some years the Best Film award has been given to the
safe and obvious choice, but in other years the choice has been
much less obvious and even surprising. Citras are highly esteemed
and widely recognized. Winners are usually identified as such in
stories, and multiple winners constitute a sort of Pantheon of
Indonesian Cinema. On the other hand, many actors and actresses
who are household names in Indonesia have never won a Citra.

THE ART OF MOVIE ADVERTISING

Movie advertising is a genre of its own. There are illustrated ads
run in newspapers, there are ads printed on glossy paper, small
and large, to be displayed in glass cases inside theaters, and there
are huge hand-painted cloth banners, several feet in dimension,
which are strung over movie theater facades or across streets. The
pictures in the ads relate vaguely to the story of the film but concentrate on the stars and eroticize the women—a favorite pose is
the actress in semirecumbent position, up on one elbow, with legs
slightly spread and breasts prominent. Such poses rarely appear in
the movies themselves. Indeed, the publicly displayed ads are considerably more erotic than the movies shown inside the theaters.

Posters are generally similar to movie ads in the West. But the
ready-made advertising copy which accompanies imported films is
too austere for Indonesian tastes, so artists are employed to redo
the ads and make them more busy. In addition to the main figures
in the ad, several production stills of scenes from the film will be
added. The result is like a modern Balinese painting—crowded
with details—or, to go back a thousand years, like the bas-reliefs
on Borobudur and other Javanese monuments from the Hindu-
Buddhist period, chock-full of people, animals, and foliage.

The printed posters are made in studios around Jakarta for distribution throughout the country. The great painted sheets, by contrast, are a more modest craft, done in small shops in the provinces, each area making its own. (It would be fascinating to learn whether different areas make different sorts of visualizations for the same film, each according to the regional culture.) Each sheet can be used a few dozen times until it is worn out by wind and weather and discarded or perhaps gets a new life as an awning on a street vendor's cart.

Comedy ads have their own convention: People's heads are huge in proportion to their bodies. There is no obvious antecedent in the Javanese shadow theater known as *wayang*. There the clowns are certainly grotesque but not with extra-large heads. This may just be a convenient artistic convention—like the compulsive fast camera zooms, in and out, in and out, so characteristic of Indonesian slapstick comedy films. It is tempting to interpret both these conventions as a harmless flirtation with disorder.

In short, the film industry in all its manifestations plays a prominent role in Indonesian life. It may be true that, relative to other Southeast Asian countries, fewer people in Indonesia actually see fewer films. But few Indonesians can avoid some contact with some aspects of films. What we could call the peripheral channels of film communication are especially fascinating: the advertising in newspapers and magazines, the huge pictures on bioskop buildings, the fashions promoted by film stars, all these different ways in which the cinema permeates Indonesian life.

CHAPTER 3

PATTERNS OF INDONESIAN CULTURE IN CINEMA

Imagine, if you can, that the only evidence we have of an otherwise unknown culture is a collection of a hundred feature films produced by its cinema industry. What can we learn about that culture? We could draw up an account of the cinematic culture we find in the films, and we could assume that it is a product of the "real" culture. But we would be hard put to determine what elements were accurate reflection, what were skewed refraction, and where the filmmakers were moving ahead of their culture in more or less conscious attempts to influence their audience. What we can be sure of is that all these different strands exist and in some complex manner bind a cinematic culture to its culture of origin.

Here our task is easier than that hypothetical puzzle in Borgesian celluloid archaeology. We can examine the Indonesian cinematic culture in reference to what we know of the Indonesian culture of origin, its shape and its ambitions, and make some progress in recognizing the many intertwined strands. And we can progress beyond the simplified question of whether a cinema reflects or shapes in order to show in detail how it does both.

The least surprising feature, and the most obviously "Indonesian," is the language. All Indonesian films use the Indonesian language almost exclusively. The exceptions are occasional words in a local language thrown in for atmospheric effect. But in the world of the movies, even long discussions in isolated Javanese villages, or around Batak dinner tables, are carried out in Indonesian. This is in reality quite unlikely. Most Indonesians, although they may well speak good Indonesian, still use a regional language— Javanese, Batak, or whatever—for domestic talk. The 1988 film

26

Tjut Nya Dien, by Eros Djarot, is in many ways a revolutionary venture. Much of the dialogue is in Acehnese with Indonesian subtitles—quite an astonishing departure from the normal procedure. But in general, Indonesian movies are in Indonesian and nothing of any significance for the plot line is entrusted to any other language. It has been said that with the advent of sound films in the 1930s, the English spoken in Great Britain and the United States began to converge rapidly because no one could afford to make films in a strikingly inaccessible regional dialect of English and because audiences began to be influenced by the relatively similar movie English or movie American which was emerging. In my own research on emotion in Indonesia, I have been impressed by the differences between Indonesian spoken by Minangkabau and Indonesian spoken by Javanese (Heider 1991). But it is likely that twenty years ago these differences would have been considerably greater.

At an early stage in this project, a leading Indonesian intellectual tried to warn me off—Indonesian films are not at all realistic, he said. In a literal ethnographic sense, of course, he was right.

Several years ago Taufiq Ismail (1977) wrote a humorous piece for *Tempo* in which he exposed the portrait that Indonesian films painted of Indonesian society. He reports that of the twenty-seven finalist films in the 1977 Film Festival Indonesia, 85.1 percent are set in cities and 14.9 percent in the country; 92.6 percent concern middle-class people and 7.4 percent concern peasants; 18.5 percent feature Mercedes or Volvo cars; 70.3 percent show at least one family with only one child and 29.7 percent have families with more than one child; 52.1 percent of the city films have nightclub scenes; in 22.2 percent of the films, economic necessity drives a woman into prostitution, but none of them ever look for honest work; 40.7 percent of the films show extramarital sex; 7.2 percent show suicide and another 14.4 percent show attempted suicide. Ten years later, Salim Said (1987) made another tally of the fifteen finalists in the 1987 Film Festival Indonesia and found much the same: The urban and middle-class emphasis was even stronger; families still overwhelmingly had only one child and no servants; and while extramarital sex was up, prostitutes were out. And finally, Said notes that there was almost no mention of religion—this in a country where, since 1965, religious affiliation has been required.

Ismail and Said are right. In terms of these features, Indonesian films certainly do not reflect Indonesian life—or, better, one should say that the bulk of the films show only the narrowest slice of urban middle-class wealthy Indonesian life and manage to distort even that. So my informant was quite right also: Indonesian films are not realistic. There is, however, one area where Indonesian feature films are almost ethnographic: in their depiction of domestic ceremonies like weddings, funerals, and even circumcision rites. The language is all Indonesian, of course, but the music for these sequences is right and the elaborate costumes are authentically regional. And even though only a few moments of a ceremony are used in a film, those are generally the peak moments of symbolic significance.

But all this is at the most obvious verbal and visual level. No one acquainted with the cinema of a country would expect any sort of statistical accuracy in ethnographic terms. The skewing of reality is often attributed to the exigencies of filmmaking—small children are notoriously difficult to direct, for example, and lots of small children can be a nightmare. Thus in movies we see one-child families in a country where even the optimistic slogan of the national family planning program is "Two Is Enough." To explain other unrealistic patterns noted by both Ismail and Said—such as why prostitutes figure prominently in 1978 but not in 1987—requires a more cultural-historical approach, to which we shall return later. Although Mercedes and Volvos are replaced by Hondas and Toyotas, and prostitutes come and prostitutes go, there are some basic cultural patterns which do remain constant.

TWO BASIC PATTERNS

Anthropological attempts to characterize entire cultures in single terms have not met with universal acclaim. Ruth Benedict tried it in 1934 in *Patterns of Culture* when she borrowed classic Greek labels from the nineteenth-century philosopher Nietzsche to describe twentieth-century tribal societies: Zuñi are "Apollonian"; Kwakiutl are "Dionysian" (and Dobu are "Paranoid"). A decade later, in thinking about Japan (*The Chrysanthemum and the Sword,* 1946), she tried again with a dichotomy between Guilt Cultures and Shame Cultures. Such attempts are too gross and too rigid to deal with the various complexities of culture, especially when we are talking not about tribes of a few hundred people but nations of many millions. There is too much variation among those many people, as well as too much inconsistency between various aspects of culture for a single unified label. And yet there is a basic insight in these formulations. Here I want to characterize "Indonesian culture" by some basic principles and contrast it with "American culture" in order to throw light on the differences between Indonesian films and Hollywood films. Certain caveats must be kept in mind: Different cultures are not totally different—there are overlaps; not all members of a culture are in accord—there are variations; the more general one gets (Indonesian instead of Minangkabau, American instead of Low Country South Carolina), the less precision is possible.

In a study of the cultural patterns of emotion in three different Indonesian cultures, I demonstrated the astonishing degree of variation in ideas about emotion within each culture (Level 1), the striking—and explainable—differences between each of the three cultures in Indonesia (Level 2), and the agreements among all three of these Indonesian cultures in contrast to American emotional patterns (Level 3). This finding is hardly surprising, but it is always necessary to emphasize the different degrees of valid consistency or agreement at the different levels. And here, talking about "Indonesian cinema," we are working at a very general level indeed—the equivalent of Level 3.

Two of these basic patterns are strikingly important when thinking about Indonesian cinema. They can best be expressed as oppositions along two continua:

Continuum I is a person's basic drive or orientation toward:

individual autonomy			social embeddedness
inner state	←――――――→	interaction
the lone individual			the family group

Continuum II is a sense that the basic conflict of life (and movie plots) is between:

| good/evil | | | order/disorder |
| good guys/bad guys | ←――→ | agents of order/agents of disorder |

Schematically speaking, Indonesian cultures (and cinema) are found toward the right end of both continua, while Western cultures (and cinema) are found toward the left end. But we are speaking here in very general terms. These are continua, not alternative categories. Moreover, we are talking about "cultures" which are far from uniform. The best representation of the situation would be to show cultures as pollywog-like figures to indicate where they put the weight of their attention:

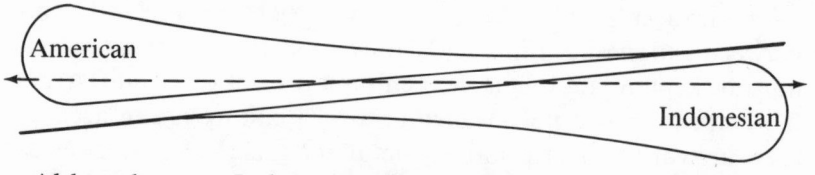

Although some Indonesian films emphasize individual autonomy at the expense of the group, the dominant Indonesian pattern, which shapes most Indonesian film plots, emphasizes the group at the expense of the individual. Conversely, there are American films (and American individuals) whose highest value is the group at the expense of the individual, but certainly it is more common for the individual to strive for personal satisfaction regardless of the interest of the group. In another sort of film study the focus would be on auteur films which go against the grain of these cultural conventions. But in this cultural analysis we shall concentrate on the more genre-like films as they embody the dominant themes of their cultures.

THE INDIVIDUAL VS. THE GROUP

Clifford Geertz, in a much-admired passage, has sketched one formulation of the self: "The Western conception of the person as a bounded, unique, more or less integrated motivational and cognitive universe, a center of awareness, emotion, judgment, and action organized into a distinctive whole and set contrastively both against other such wholes and against its social and natural background, is, however incorrigible it may seem to us, a rather peculiar idea within the context of the world's cultures" (1983:59). This Western ideal, the dominant version of the person, is realized in Western cinema in various ways: The emphasis is on the individual, families are relatively unimportant, the individual works out an individual fate. For Indonesians, who place more value on the health of the group, this blatant individualism seems peculiarly selfish.

These patterns are not proclaimed in the abstract by some entity called "culture," but they are evinced in the many thousands of acts of life. Marriage arrangements are particularly diagnostic: They present a nontrivial problem which every culture must resolve with a limited range of possibilities. In America today the ideal marriage is arranged by the bride and groom responding to their mutual inner emotional states. Families should not "interfere"; the couple should be "happy" and "in love." In Indonesia today marriages are more likely to be arranged by negotiations between leaders of families or descent groups of the couple. The inner emotional states of the principals are not prime considerations. There are many exceptions to this rule, notably lower-class Indonesians, people making second marriages, and people living in cities apart from their homes of origin.

No good statistics on this issue come to hand from Indonesia, but Walter Edwards, in his study of Japanese marriages (1989), paints a similar picture and cites studies which suggest that about a third of the marriages are arranged by families. Apparently Indonesia, like Japan, is in transition with a mix of wedding arrangement patterns. The Western transition period was well described in novels, plays, and operas from the time of Shakespeare through the nineteenth century. For example, the plot of *Romeo and Juliet* hinges on this conflict. The two principals want to arrange their own marriage, their families object, and tragedy results. But by the mid-twentieth century American marriages were entirely in the hands of the boy and the girl, and no credible movie plot could include a family-arranged marriage.

But patterns at either end of the continuum, both the socially embedded and the autonomous, are complex and each contains something of the other. Herbert Gans, writing about "Middle American individualism," describes the "search for . . . liberation from unwelcome cultural, social, political, and economic constraints, but also from lack of economic as well as emotional security . . . to avoid involuntary conformity . . . [and] to sidestep obligatory membership in institutions and organizations, sacred and secular" (1988:2). Gans stresses that individualism does not simply mean social isolation. Rather, it means a freedom within a noncoercive set "of family, friends, and informal relations and groups" (1988:4). And, conversely, Indonesia is not simply group-oriented. Much of the literature, including films, in concerned with conflicts between the interests of an individual and the concerns of the group.

A comparison of emotions illustrates this complexity. Emotions are at once inner states and externally expressed acts of communication. On the whole, recent research has revealed a tendency for Westerners to think of emotions as inner states, while others elsewhere think of emotions more at the service of interaction. A precisely calibrated example comes from my study of emotion in Sumatra (Heider 1991). The Minangkabau, who are bilingual in their regional language (Minangkabau) and in the national language (Indonesian), provided scenarios for emotions in each language. Indonesian is the language they employ in cosmopolitan settings, at school, in the markets, and on the national scene, and so I hypothesized that emotions in Indonesian would fall more toward the Western, individualistic, end of the spectrum. Further, it seemed that the same people thinking about emotions in their home language, Minangkabau, would produce more interaction scenarios. For the Minangkabau it turns out that "happiness" is the result of good luck and gifts from others, for example, while for the same people, thinking in Indonesian, "happiness" is the result of personal achievement.

Direct translations from English to Indonesian are even more revealing. These show a strong shift from English-language inner state concerns to Indonesian interaction concerns. Here is a sample from one of many Indonesian translations of Shakespeare (*Hamlet,* act I, scene 1, on the castle ramparts):

MARCELLUS: Farewell, honest soldier.

But in Indonesian it is:

MARCELLUS: O, s'lamat malam, kawanku. ("Oh, good night, my friend.")

"Honest soldier" refers to the inner state or quality of the person; but *"kawanku"* is a relationship term, almost a kinship term, meaning "my friend" or "my comrade." In the English, Marcellus comments on the guard's inner quality of honesty. There is of course an Indonesian word for honesty, and the translator could well have rendered the line *"serdadu jujur,"* the literal meaning of "honest soldier." Perhaps it would have sounded a bit strange, implying somehow that the guard was not taking bribes. But in fact the translator dodged the issue completely, instead commenting on the relationship between Marcellus and the guard: "my comrade."

There used to be a bilingual sign hanging over the exit of the Bukittinggi (West Sumatra) museum. In Indonesian it read: Terimakasih Atas Kunjungan Anda, which means "thank you for your visit." But in English it read: Thank You for Your Interest. Thus in Indonesian it was commenting on a social interaction, while the English was stressing an inner attitude.

The film *Rebel Without a Cause* was distributed in Indonesia with Indonesian-language subtitles. In one scene, James Dean kisses Natalie Wood, who expresses surprise:

WOOD: Why did you do that?
DEAN: Cause I felt like it.

But in fact the translator just gives up on this inner state confession and has Dean answer, "Aku tidak tahu," I don't know.

In the Cornell Indonesian-language lessons (Oetomo, Fietkiewicz, and Wolff 1984:1), Lesson One, Basic Sentences, we find:

1a. Good Evening, Tuti.   Selamat Sore, Bu Tuti.
 b. How are you?   Apa Kabar? (What's the news?)
2a. Fine.   Kabar Baik. (The news is good.)

This is a cultural, not a literal, translation. We are of course dealing with greeting formulas. But nevertheless, the pattern holds true. In English one asks about an inner condition. In Indonesian one asks about the world events.

A cultural anthropology text (Ember and Ember 1990:3) has a section titled "The Anthropological Curiosity" in which the authors discuss what motivates anthropologists to go study other peoples. When this chapter appeared in Indonesian (Ihromi [1980: 4]), the title read "Hal-hal Yang Ingin Diketahui Dalam Antropologi"—which certainly does not refer to an inner state of curiosity and can be roughly translated as "Things That Need to Be Known About in Anthropology."

There is a story which the prominent Indonesian scholar Ben Anderson tells on himself. In one of his first attempts at translation, he rendered the title of a short story, "Sensasi di Atas Pohon Kelapa," as "Sensations Felt at the Top of the Coconut Tree." In fact, the Indonesian author did not intend a comment on the inner state of the person who had climbed to the top of the palm but was alluding to "The Sensational Events Which Occurred at the Top of the Coconut Tree." But Anderson, a Westerner, had opted for the inner state translation of the ambiguous word *sensasi*.

These translation examples illustrate a process of "making more social," or "less individualistic." Rita Kipp (1984) provides quite a different example in her description of Karo Batak (North Sumatra) relationship terms. She describes the process of *erturtur,* "making a relationship," in which two strangers work out more or less fictive genealogical ties that will allow them to use kinship terms for each other. This is far more than the casual American pattern of, say, metaphorically calling a friend of the family "Uncle George." The Karo practice turns strangers into kin.

From these anecdotes and examples we move to general statements about a culturally varied nation of 175 million people. For some purposes such generalizations would be hopelessly inaccurate. But we are thinking here about Indonesian movies, which themselves are comparable generalizations. They are made in a set form to be shown to those 175 million people across the archipelago and hence must attempt to hit the cultural median.

ORDER VS. DISORDER

A second broad but useful generalization concerns the basic moral conflict of a culture. The West is concerned with the opposition of good vs. evil, while Indonesia emphasizes order vs. disorder. This is in no way to imply that the West ignores disorder or that Indonesians do not know evil. But the dominant concerns are different. Japan shares the Indonesian concern with order, and the transformation of Shakespeare's *King Lear* into Japanese is revealing. This masterpiece inevitably comes to mind if one thinks of Western dramatizations of disorder. The king violates the social order by abdicating; two of his daughters violate the family order by savaging their father; he, likewise, violates family order by rejecting his one honest daughter; and so on—the human as well as the natural world is cast into disorder. But even here, in the ultimate exploration of disorder, Shakespeare must attend to the good/evil theme and make Lear a *good* man who triggers all manner of disorder. It is a remarkable balancing act for the playwright.

In Japan there is no such constraint. The Japanese director Akiro Kurosawa made a film version of *King Lear,* and it turned out to be much more pervasively about disorder. Even the Japanese title, *Ran,* means disorder. The Japanese lord creates much more disorder: Not only does he renounce his official duties by dividing his lands up among his children, but he also slaughters his in-laws in violation of his obligations of hospitality. For a Western audience, Hidetoshi's obvious wickedness loses him all sympathy. Shakespeare had to temper Lear's disorderliness with goodness; Kurosawa can ignore good and evil and go all-out with disorderly actions.

As we shall see, Indonesian movies are overwhelmingly concerned with order and disorder. This poses a major cultural barrier for Western viewers. In Indonesian movies there are characters who drive the plot—even trigger the main action—by some act which has negative consequences for others. The main plot then deals with the attempts of others to resolve the problem and restore relations to the previous state. They usually succeed, and in the end everyone is happily reunited. Including the original troublemaker.

The Western viewer who reads this sort of plot as involving a bad guy and some good guys can follow events comfortably right up to the conclusion. But then where is the denouement, where the triumph of good, where the punishment of evil, the wages of sin? And why, above all, is the bad guy, suddenly converted to virtue, now joyfully accepted by those whom he has wronged? The answer is that Indonesian movies do not have bad guys. (I am of course trapped in American cowboy film talk—many of these Indonesian troublemakers are actually women.) The Indonesian figures create disorder, confusion, chaos. They have done something wrong, bad, evil. (Indonesian languages have many words for these ideas.) But they are not inherently bad. We can best label them "agents of disorder." They can be converted and order can be restored. (And the uneasy Westerner still asks: "All is forgiven?")

Order and disorder. This is the key to much of Indonesian life.

It shows up in the most common hortatory messages on govern-
ment-sponsored signs and billboards: BE ORDERLY. Most per-
tinently here, it is already the guiding principle of the traditional
Javanese *wayang* shadow puppet play. These dramas, which figure
strongly in Indonesian life far beyond the confines of Central
Java, are taken from the Hindu epics, the *Mahabharata* and the
Ramayana. A single puppeteer works the hundreds of puppets
during the hours-long performance, sings all the parts, and leads
the gamelan orchestra and chorus. The puppets themselves are cut
and painted sheets of water buffalo hide. The figures—gods, god-
desses, giants, clowns, and more—are portrayed asymmetrically
in profile. But the drama opens with a single figure—not of a
player but of the great World Tree, which is bilaterally symmetrical. It is called *gunungan,* meaning "mountain," and symbolizes
the universe in order. When it is removed the action begins. Chaos
is created by the disorderly armies at the left hand of the puppeteer
and is eventually resolved by the forces of order at his right hand.
When armies, puppeteer, and audience are finally exhausted and
once again in order, the symmetrical *gunungan* is again planted at
center stage and the play is over.

But even limiting the discussion to *wayang* only, the claim that
order vs. disorder is more important than good vs. evil is open to
debate. Several times I have brought the matter up to groups of
well-informed Indonesians and have seen the matter hotly de-
bated. The literature shows a similar lack of consensus. In writing
about *wayang,* for example, Clifford Geertz has pointed out that
"the immediate impulse is to call the Pendawas, who are certainly
heroes, the 'good' men and Korawas, who are not quite so clearly
villains, the 'bad' men; but to identify the figures in the drama as
though they were characters in a medieval morality play would be
a serious misunderstanding" (1960:270). Geertz claimed that "the
struggle is not between good and evil, . . . but between the old
opposites of *kasar* and *halus* feelings, between base animal passion and detached, effortless self-control" (1960:270).

Benedict Anderson spoke of the "moral pluralism" of *wayang*
but suggested that "recently, under Christian, European influences, probably dating back to the end of the last century, there
has been a tendency in Java to simplify the older, complicated
interrelationships. Tolerance of ambiguity has begun to decline,
and *wayang* has tended to be devalued towards a commonplace

morality play between Good and Evil" (1965:6). Anderson followed this observation with a footnote: "This kind of interpretation has unluckily been encouraged by transient foreign commentators, who have too often imposed their own moral conceptions on a tradition they failed fully to comprehend" (1965:6, n. 1).

Barbara Hatley expands this line of thought beyond *wayang* to other genres: "In every performance there is movement out from the plenitude and splendor of a palace into chaos and conflict in forest and foreign land then finally back to a palace setting, with order restored and nothing of significance changed. What is not generally recognized is the fact that these dramatic elements and the social/cultural assumptions they express are not exclusive to wayang, but form a common store, a shared dramatic tradition for all forms of traditional Javanese theatre" (1981:19, 20).

In his study of the urban folk theater *ludruk* in East Java, James Peacock distinguishes between traditional and modern plots. The traditional plot (T-plot) sounds much like *wayang:* "No T-plot villain sustains a movement toward a final-scene punishment. The T-plot moves more toward harmonizing the group than toward punishing an individual or fulfilling an individual's aim" (1987:138). Shelly Errington, drawing inspiration from Javanese *wayang,* emphasizes the order/disorder theme in her treatment of politics and ritual in southern Sulawesi. She goes on to say that "the image of the orderly polity—in which everyone enacts his or her place and nothing disturbs the realization of that order—is a powerful one in the political and artistic forms (which are the same thing) of the ranked polities of Southeast Asia" (1989:275). And Jane Wellenkamp, another anthropologist working in Sulawesi, emphasizes "order and disorder in Toraja thought and ritual" (1988).

But James Brandon, who in general concurs with the interpretations of *wayang* mentioned above, says there is no doubt about the nature of conflict between Pandawa and ogres—it is "unequivocally between good and evil" (1970:20). And Ward Keeler, who recently studied *wayang* in Central Java, can write: "Contemporary Javanese commentary sees the Kurawa as unequivocally evil, given over to their envy, lust for power and coarseness, and the Pandhawa as good, models of fairness, potency, and patience. Their struggle is therefore the eternal one between good and evil" (1987:243).

The resolution of these differences is to recognize that order/ disorder and good/evil are alternative frames for interpreting plot and motivation in Indonesian films. And in this book I shall develop the case for order/disorder by demonstrating that it accounts for much that a good/evil opposition leaves mystifying.

Wayang, because it is the most famous dramatic genre of the dominant ethnic group in Indonesia and so strongly exemplifies the concern for order, comes in handy as an antecedent for Indonesian movies. But the truth is that order, rather than goodness, is the prime moral imperative throughout Indonesia. And in fact most of the early Indonesian filmmakers and many of the present ones are not even Javanese, yet they too are concerned with order. As we shall see, signs of order and disorder pervade these films in major and minor ways. And the troublemakers act and are treated in an Indonesian fashion. What they do is described in terms of disorder. Sometimes one might want to question whether an act is bad, or disorderly, or both. The key, I think, is in the outcome: Was the perpetrator punished or was order restored? It is worth noting, too, that in the cognitive maps of three Indonesian languages (Heider 1991) the emotions of disorder occupy a major space. In English, words like "confusion" are barely recognized as emotions at all. But their Indonesian and Minangkabau equivalents (like *kacau* and *bingung*) are unquestionably emotions, and important ones at that.

Finally, we can take a stab at defining the Indonesian national culture that is presented in these films—all the while thinking of which elements have traditional roots and which seem to look toward a possible, emerging, future. First we note that in the films people speak Indonesian. Religions, regional cultures, and regional languages are recognizable but only as identifying marks, not as important motivating aspects of people's lives. Modern homes, appliances, clothing, and automobiles are much in evidence. But the core Indonesian values of group harmony and order are still dominant. In broad outlines *this* is what national Indonesian cinematic culture looks like, what the more formulaic films portray, and what the more auteur-like films play against. Now, with these very basic and pervasive cultural principles in mind, we can proceed to the films themselves.

CHAPTER 4

GENRES, PLOTS, AND TALE TYPES

When Indonesians talk about types of films, they tend to use Western loanwords, beginning, of course, with the very word "film." The major division of films is between "Film Cerita" and "Film Non-Cerita"—the word *cerita* means "fictional story." Thus "Film Cerita" is somewhat more descriptive than its English equivalent, "feature film." "Film Non-Cerita" refers to everything else, especially documentary films.

GENRES

Various genres—the Indonesian word is *jenis,* from genus—are commonly recognized in Indonesia and, again, the labels are usually loanwords. There is no authoritative Indonesian list, but the usual sorts of terms used are Action, Silat, Mistik, Komedi, Legend, Suspense, Horror, and Drama. These words are European, despite the availability of Indonesian words which have appropriate meanings. The exception is Silat, which is used for the Indonesian versions of the general East Asian martial arts.

Here I shall suggest various genres and types into which most Indonesian films will fit comfortably. By genre I mean a recognizable film prototype with a standard setting, time period, plot, and the presence or absence of violence, sadistic sexuality, and supernatural powers. In addition to these clear genres, there are also types of films which may have some features in common but are not, in such a clear sense, genres. They may be films about the struggle against the Dutch (1945–1949), for example, which are by necessity somewhat similar but do not have enough of the basic similarities to warrant talking about a genre prototype. The films which fall between my rather obvious genre categories would be especially interesting to examine. They might say a lot about new emerging genres or about individual filmmakers' resistance and innovation.

Legend Genre

These films are dramatizations of traditional legends or folktales, usually Javanese or Sundanese, and are usually set in the Hindu-Buddhist or early Muslim period, circa A.D. 1000 to the seventeenth century A.D. (see Danandjaja 1984:66 ff.) They are related to the various sorts of *wayang* performances of Java but lack the refined dance and movements of courtly *wayang*. The main protagonists usually have supernatural powers used in fighting, transformations, and flying—all of which are much more effectively portrayed by cinematic technology than would ever be possible on stage.

Lutung Kasarung is a Sundanese legend about a magical monkey who abducts a princess and eventually is turned into a man by her love; *Ratu Pantai Selatan* (The Princess of the Southern Sea) is a modernized retelling of the story of the princess who lives beneath the ocean and falls in love with a mortal; *Loro Jonggrang* tells about the princess who says she will only marry the usurper of her father's throne if he builds a thousand temples before sunrise, then tricks him into stopping with the nine hundred and ninety-ninth and is turned into stone for her treachery. And *Roro Mendut* (1983) is about another princess who is awarded as booty to a victor, resists him, and eventually runs off with her true love. *Saur Sepuh,* the blockbuster film of 1988, features a huge mechanical bird and great battle scenes strongly reminiscent of those in the Japanese film *Ran* but with elephants. These are costume dramas, historical legends, or legendary history, telling stories which are familiar throughout Indonesia. Although popular, the films rarely get much critical attention.

Kompeni Genre

Kompeni Genre films deal with the Dutch colonial period in the archipelago, roughly from the seventeenth century until the late nineteenth century. The Dutch East India Company—the Verenigde Oost-Indische Compagnie—although it was actually disbanded at the end of the eighteenth century, is the embodiment of the entire period. Its logo, the intertwined initials VOC and the red, white, and blue stripes of the Dutch flag, is readily recognizable. The Kompeni is to the colonial period somewhat as the Seventh Cavalry is to the frontier in American westerns: based on history but used iconically. Historical gears often slip in movies, and the VOC may be juxtaposed to the Padri Wars of the early nineteenth century with costumes and technology which look suspiciously late nineteenth century.

This is less of a cohesive genre than are some others. I use the label Kompeni films for several films with colonial period settings which tell of conflict between Dutch and Indonesians. The prototypical plot pits the eponymous hero *(Jaka Gledek, Jaka Sembung, Pak Sakerah)* against the Dutch forces. The immediate issue is usually heavy tax demands on the part of the Dutch. There is a fair amount of unrestrained sadism—gouging out of eyes, torturing of prisoners, and the like. Sadistic sexuality—Dutch soldiers raping village girls—is common. The hero usually has supernatural powers (*ilmu,* or mystical knowledge) which have been given him by a Muslim teacher and which he uses to protect the villagers. In one film, *Jaka Sembung,* the Dutch also use offensive magic when they employ a *dukun* (magician) to raise a headless corpse who is to capture the rebellious Jaka Sembung.

The hero is often aided by a woman, either a villager or the daughter of a Dutch officer. These films end in a sort of dilemma. Although the hero is triumphant, usually he and his women are dead. We know that Dutch rule has decades more to run, yet the Dutch are repulsed from that particular village. It is a local triumph at best. James Peacock (1987:286) has given a detailed description of *Pak Sakerah* which was presented as a *ludruk* melodrama in Surabaya in 1963. Although the play and the film are obviously related, each is true to its medium. The play has sequences of low humor, lacks supernatural maneuvers, and though set in the early twentieth century seems to be less about conflict with the Dutch than about the domestic problems of Pak Sakerah. The film, like the play, opens in a Surabaya sugar factory but has been shaped to fit the Kompeni genre. The Dutch are oppressing people with their taxation demands, and Pak Sakerah, a rather bloodthirsty fellow, uses his magical powers to protect the people but is eventually hanged by the Dutch after giving a rousing speech about freedom. Thus, whatever the original source of the Pak Sakerah story, the *ludruk* players have made it *ludruk* and the filmmakers have turned it into a Kompeni film.

Two recent and highly acclaimed films are set in the same period but are noteworthy because they do not nicely fit the Kompeni genre. *November 1828,* by Teguh Karya, is a fictional story of an event in a Javanese village during the Javanese wars between the Dutch and the forces of the hero Diponogoro. *Tjut Nya Dien,* by Eros Djarot, is a historical film about the Acehnese Wars at the turn of the century. These two efforts are clearly auteur films, eschewing the plots, the magic, and the sadistic sex of the Kompeni films, yet they have emerged from the Kompeni genre. Both of them won several Citras.

Japanese Period Genre

Japanese Period films are another minor genre. They are set in the three-and-a-half-year period of the Japanese occupation (1942–1945). The standard plot involves an Indonesian woman who is abducted and humiliated by the Japanese army. She winds up in a prison camp or as a concubine/servant of the Japanese. There is one honorable Japanese officer, however, and they fall in love, but at the end of the war (usually marked by a stock shot of the atomic cloud over Hiroshima) he commits suicide. This genre has even more sadistic violence than do the Kompeni films, and the Japanese soldiers are much more brutal than the Dutch. Sexual sadism —rape and other abuse—is especially prominent in these films. Female nakedness is standard but only as part of the violence, never as a consequence of love. Some of these films, like *Kamp Tawanan Wanita* (Women's Prison Camp) and *Budak Nafsu* (Slave of Passion), are little more than sex exploitation vehicles, while *Lebak Membara* (Lebak in Flames) and *Kadarwati* have slightly higher ambitions. The focus is usually on the abuses suffered by the Indonesian women, although Indonesian men are often in the background as guerrillas fighting the Japanese.

Perjuangan Genre

The Perjuangan ("Struggle") period runs from the end of World War II when the defeated Japanese forces withdrew from the archipelago until December 1949 when the Dutch gave up their claims to the islands. This was the period when Indonesians were fighting for their independence. Although there have been many films about the Perjuangan, they might better be considered as historical statements rather than examples of a particular genre. Even in the 1980s many of the main figures in the Struggle were still alive and active, most notably among them the president of the republic, Suharto. The mandate of every Indonesian government ment rests firmly on the events of the Struggle. In this sense, this period is still too immediately important to allow it to be taken over by genre films. Later, in Chapter 10, we shall examine some of these films from a historical point of view for what they reveal about the past and what they show of present thinking about the past (See also Said 1990).

Sentimental Genre

This is the most important genre of Indonesian films for many reasons. In Indonesian it is called "drama" and sometimes it is subdivided into Drama Rumah Tangga (domestic drama) and Drama SMA (high school drama) or Drama Remaja (youth drama). It has been called, simply, melodrama. The classic sentimental plot, discussed in detail below, has roots in the old Malay *kaba,* the traditional epic tales which were first written down at the turn of the century. It exemplifies both of the basic Indonesian cultural patterns I introduced in Chapter 3: the interaction (or social embeddedness) as well as the concern with order and disorder, albeit on a domestic scale. There is usually no sensuality and certainly no supernatural power at play. Violence is limited to the disciplining of children. These films have contemporary settings, usually involving rich Jakarta families. Where religion is hinted at, it is as likely to be Christianity as Islam. From the standpoint of cultural analysis the Sentimental genre films are the most thoroughly Indonesian, but their melodramatic tone makes it hard for intellectuals, Indonesian or Western, to take them seriously.

Horror Genre

Horror films are one of the most common types. Although they are set in the present, they do resemble the Legend genre films in their strong roots in traditional Indonesian folk beliefs, especially those involving supernatural powers. The basic theme begins with the creation of a supernatural monster of some sort who then threatens humans and is eventually subdued by a superior super-natural power, usually knowledge *(ilmu)*, taught to the hero by a guru. These films make extensive use of cinematic technology for their gruesome special effects. Crudely sadistic sexuality is even more prominent in these films than in any but the Japanese Period films.

Traditional folklore is often the basis of the plot. In *Buaya Putih* (The White Crocodile) there is the traditional theme of the two students of the guru, one using his knowledge for good, the other to disrupt social relationships. There are two generations of were-crocodiles (complete with an erotic underwater rape sequence). Suzzanna, a prominent actress, has starred in a series of films about a Sundelbolong, a supernatural woman raised from the dead, identified by a great gruesome hole in her back, who is avenger and destroyer (see Danandjaja 1984:71).

Although these Horror films use certain techniques similar to those of Western horror films, they always involve supernatural monsters, never simply natural humans with a violent bent. When I saw one of Suzzanna's Sundelbolong films in a Jakarta theater—it was *Malam Satu Suro,* roughly translatable as "Friday the Thir-teenth"—I was soon surrounded by youths who pointed out paral-lels to American horror films like *Nightmare on Elm Street,* also a favorite in Jakarta. In the Sundelbolong film there was a scene in a graveyard at night where a man was attacked by a snake and a frog. The audience laughed uproariously. It was real laughter, not nervous release. This sort of horribly humorous scene is common in the Horror genre films, although at first, when I was watching the movies alone at home, I misjudged their emotional tone and completely missed the humor.

Other Categories

There are several other useful categories of film in the Indonesian repertory, some of which are recognized by Indonesians and some based on American types. Although I would hesitate to call them genres of film, since they do not have common plots, they are worth mentioning as types.

Komedi. Many films marked by flippant titles and outsized heads in their cartoon ads are comedies, relying on visual slapstick as well as verbal joking.

Expedition Films. In these films an ethnographic expedition or a development team wanders into an exotic and usually sinister "primitive tribe." These films are set in Irian Jaya or Sumatra (but apparently are filmed outside Jakarta).

Musicals. Films following the Indian pattern of breaking the action to allow the star to sing hit songs are not common, but singers like Rhoma Irama have made them (see Frederick 1985).

Anak-Anak: Kid Films. These are films *about* children, not necessarily aimed at children. Indeed, there are short films, live as well as animated, which are made for late afternoon television showing: *Si Unyil,* a popular animated puppet series, follows the adventures of the little boy Unyil in his uplifting encounters with peers and adults. But there are also feature films which deal with children's problems in the adult world. The first famous one was *Si Doel Anak Betawi* (Doel—The Betawi Kid), which introduced Rano Karno, now a major adult actor. The parallel to the 1930s Shirley Temple films is close. Some films of fixed genres also deal with children. *Buah Hati Mama* (Mama's Sweetheart) is a prototypical Sentimental genre film. *Arie Hanggara,* which packed in the youthful Bukittinggi audiences at the end of the fasting month in 1986, was the dramatization of an actual case of child abuse and death which had dominated the newspapers of the year before.

Miscellanea. There are also a few films dealing with social problems such as prostitution *(Ponirah Terpadana),* ethnic conflict *(Putri Giok),* and crime *(Carok,* a *Godfather*-like film set in Madura). There are, as well, Indonesian remakes of American films: *Pengantin Pantai Biru* (The Bride of the Blue Shore) from *The Blue Lagoon; Kupu Kupu Putih* (The White Butterfly) from *Rocky;* and some *Rambo* imitations.

The Uses of Genre

These, then, are some of the Indonesian film genres—types of films which "tell familiar stories with familiar characters in familiar situations" (Grant 1986:xi). Genres are overdetermined categories: groups of films which are similar in many different respects. American westerns not only have basically similar plots, for example, but also are fairly limited to a certain place, a certain time, and involve certain classes and occupations of people. (See, for example, Wright 1975.) A film cannot trifle too much with these common features and still retain genre membership. Yet playing intellectual games with the idea of genres can illuminate both film and category—consider, for example, *The Name of the Rose* as a western which happens to be set in medieval Italy.

PLOTS AND TALE TYPES

The next step is to explore plots which appear at a deeper level and are not necessarily bound to a particular genre. Using the terminology of folklore studies, we can call them tale types. (See, for example, Propp 1968; Thompson 1977; Dundes 1965; and Danandjaya 1984.) We shall look at two of these tale types. The first can be called "Female Captive Loved by Alien Male Captor." It appears in several genres, and in various guises it is familiar from European tales. The second is the classic sentimental plot, which is particular to the Sentimental genre but echoes across the entire spectrum of genres.

A Classic Tale Type: Female Captive Loved by Alien Male Captor

This plot is summarized in the title. It appears in the following form:

1. Attractive young woman
2. In distant setting
3. With alien (very different sort of male)
4. One or both rescues/saves/nurtures the other
5. He is in love with her, she may come to reciprocate
6. He is redeemed or damned

Lutung Kasarung is a Legend film based on a Sundanese legend (from western Java). The princess is poisoned by her jealous step-mother the queen with a disfiguring potion and then abandoned in the forest. The *lutung,* a black monkey, rescues her, takes her to his tree house, and restores her beauty; when she professes her love for him, he transforms into a handsome prince. Subsequently he switches back and forth between monkey and prince and eventually takes her back to the court where they marry and reign together.

Johanna is a Kompeni film which opens in a Javanese village. The Dutch force the villagers to grow coffee on pain of death. The hero vows to help the villagers resist, but when the Dutch kill his girlfriend, he takes revenge by kidnapping Johanna, the daughter of a Dutch officer. She resists, tries to run away, drops pieces of her clothing along the path to signal her rescuers. But despite her stratagems, he manages to take her to his tree house deep in the jungle. He saves her from a snake, a fever, three thugs, and a tiger; she saves him when the tiger's scratches get infected. They fall in love, formally introduce themselves, and begin an idyllic life together in the jungle. She becomes pregnant, they return to the Dutch fort, and after a long battle the final freeze frame shows Johanna, her father, and the hero walking off the battlefield united.

Japanese Period films have elements of this plot as well. *Kadarwati* is about a young woman who is lured to Singapore by the Japanese in 1942 thinking that she will be trained to be a doctor. Instead she is raped by Japanese soldiers and given to their officer, Harada, as his servant. They fall in love, she gets pregnant, he takes responsibility for a guerrilla raid, and commits suicide. In *Budak Nafsu* (Slave of Passion), Fatimah is part of a group of Indonesian women rounded up to be prostitutes for the Japanese soldiers, but she is protected by Takashi, a Japanese officer with a Ph.D. in biology. They fall in love, Fatimah is discovered helping guerrillas, Takashi lets her escape, and then commits suicide. In *Lembak Muara,* also, the good Japanese officer saves the Indonesian girl from rape; in *Kamp Tawanan Wanita* (Women's Prison Camp) Armelia is brutalized, caught trying to escape, and rescued by Lt. Nakamura, who keeps her as his servant. They fall in love, she gets pregnant, and in a final prison break Nakamura commits suicide.

The first part of this theme—where the woman is at the mercy of the alien captor—is familiar in European and American films as well. Indeed, it occurs throughout the Western literary tradition, but here we shall restrict the discussion to that part of the canon which emerges in cinema. *The Hunchback of Notre Dame,* a 1831 novel by Victor Hugo, had its most famous film incarnation in the 1939 American film starring Charles Laughton (pace Lon Chaney 1922). Quasimodo, the horribly deformed bell ringer at the cathedral of Notre Dame in fifteenth-century Paris, falls in love with the gypsy dancer Esmeralda. He tries to abduct her and is sentenced to a severe whipping on the public pillory. Taking pity on him, Esmeralda offers him water. When she is sentenced to be hanged for a (supposed) murder, Quasimodo rescues her and keeps her in the sanctuary of the cathedral. She pities him but does not return his love. In the end, she is pardoned by the king and goes off with Gringoire the young poet, leaving Quasimodo alone on the bell tower with a gargoyle as ugly as himself.

We are dealing just with films, of course, and quite deliberately ignoring much else of relevance. But it is necessary to at least point out that in Hugo's novel, one century older and one culture away, Esmeralda is saved, only to be finally hanged, and Quasimodo creeps into the vault where her body was placed, there to die quietly in her arms. As Wolfenstein and Leites have pointed out (1950:296–298), American films tend to have happy endings while French films do not. This principle explains the differences between the two versions of *The Hunchback.*

In *King Kong* (1933) the alien is a huge ape living on an island off the coast of Sumatra. Ann, a starving young woman in New York, is signed on to a documentary film expedition hours before the ship sails. Once at the island, Ann is abducted by the natives and given to Kong. She escapes, but Kong is captured and taken to New York, where he escapes and again abducts Ann. He loves her, or desires her in his apish way and handles her erotically, although of course the biological and cultural differences between them make a genuine relationship impossible. Finally he is killed by air force planes at the top of the Empire State Building.

In *Walkabout,* an Australian film, the young girl and her brother are lost in the desolate outback. The alien, ironically enough, is an aborigine (the least alien of all Australians). He finds the brother and sister, saves them with food and water, and leads them to safety. He falls in love with the girl, tries to

approach, perhaps to rape her, and eventually expires, crucified, on a thorn tree.

Beauty and the Beast, a French film by Jean Cocteau, is based on the European fairytale. Belle, the good daughter, goes to live with the Beast in his enchanted mansion in order to save the life of her father, a merchant. She refuses his offer of marriage. He allows her to visit her sick father on condition that she return in a week. When she does not return, he sickens and is on the brink of death when she arrives and gives him a loving look. He is transformed into a handsome prince (her dress has become steadily more regal throughout the film) and they fly off into the night sky together.

The common features of these films, Indonesian as well as European, are summarized in Table 2. Some patterns emerge. In the European examples there is one set—we can call it the King Kong model—in which the woman is of low status, does not reciprocate the alien's love, and then he dies or is abandoned. In the other European pattern—the Beauty and the Beast model—she is of high status, does return his love, and thus redeems him. (Other examples of this model are Wagner's opera *The Flying Dutchman* and the fairytale of the Frog Prince.)

The Indonesian examples do not include any of the King Kong model. In the Indonesian films, the woman is always of middle to high status, she does return the man's love, and he is redeemed. (Although in the special case of the Japanese Period films, the good Japanese officer is redeemed in death by ritual suicide.) But beyond noting that Indonesians play variations on the same basic narrative elements as Europeans, can we discern with any confidence a cultural basis for differences? The Beauty and the Beast model—the high-status woman who redeems her alien captor by her love—occurs in both traditions. It is the King Kong model, common in the West, absent in Indonesia, which offers cultural insight: Why is it absent in Indonesian cinema or, conversely, why is it so prominent in Western plots?

This may be a question without an answer, but let us make a couple of tries at it. These European aliens who are spurned by the women are far more alien than those, both European and Indonesian, who are loved. The grotesquely ugly hunchback, the monstrous primate, and the savage black man are all, by conventional European standards, impossible mates and beyond the possibility

Table 2. Common Features of "Female Captive" Films

Film	Status of Woman	Abducted or Rescued?	Locale	Male	Does She Reciprocate Attraction?	Denouement
Lutung Kasarung	high	rescued	jungle	monkey	yes	redeems him
Johanna	high	abducted	jungle	guerrilla	yes	returns him to civilization
Japanese Period films	medium	abducted by soldiers		good officer	yes	he commits suicide
Hunchback of Notre Dame	low	1. almost abducted 2. saved	cathedral	hunchback	no	he is abandoned
King Kong	low	1. abducted by natives 2. abducted by King Kong 3. abducted by King Kong	village jungle Empire State Bldg.	ape	no	he is killed
Walkabout	medium	saved	outback	aborigine	no	he expires
Beauty and the Beast	high	voluntary sacrifice	enchanted mansion	beast	yes	he becomes prince

of redemption. They have presumed to love women who, however lowly in European terms, are still far above them. We see here a concern with sexual threat to women from The Other in the form of a powerful male who must be rejected and destroyed. Both the ape in *King Kong* and the aborigine in *Walkabout* are displayed with arms outstretched, crucified. It is hard not to understand these images as referring to Christ and perhaps functioning as a softening disavowal on the part of the filmmakers, even as they build their films on the racial fears of their cultures.

A second interpretation, not unrelated to the first, uses the distinction between Indonesian order and Western evil. The Indonesian pattern here, as well as the Beauty and the Beast model, both follow the course:

CONDITION OF ORDER

The woman is first seen comfortably in her proper social setting.

CONDITION OF DISORDER

Now the woman is moved out of her social setting into a strange and unpleasant one. An apparently inappropriate male is attracted to her, loves her, and wants to marry her.

RECREATION OF ORDER

The woman's love for the alien male restores/returns/transforms him, and the two lovers reenter her social order.

In the special case of the Japanese Period films, a moral (but not a social) order is restored. Because of the exigencies of war, plus the ethnographic peculiarities of the Japanese, the good officer commits seppuku and dies.

The peculiarities of the King Kong plot, which is not found in Indonesia, are due to a concern with evil and its punishment and only secondarily with disorder. The distinguishing feature of the King Kong plot is not merely that the alien male's love is rejected by the woman, but that he is punished by death or abandonment. He has been disorderly, of course, in presuming to love above his station. But more significantly, he has committed a crime and must be punished for it. We could indeed interpret the behavior of the Indonesian alien males, as well as that of the Beast, as involving serious crimes, but that is not the main concern of this sort of plot. The strongest evidence for this argument is the fact that they are not punished. In discussing the next tale type, we shall see how important punishment or lack of it looms. But we have gone far afield and these speculations should not distract us from the main point—namely, that Indonesians play with some of the same themes of female captive, saved and loved by the alien male, as do Europeans.

The Classic Sentimental Plot: Family Separation and Reunion

The most common plot of Indonesian movies—especially the Sentimental genre movies—is the story of family and order triumphant. The prototypical plot begins and ends with the family together in a state of social order. This recalls the Javanese *wayang* performances, which use the figure of the symmetrical World Tree/Mountain to frame the cosmic battles of the plot. A. L. Becker (1979) has pointed out how the *wayang* plot begins in a royal court, proceeds to a natural setting, and ends up again at the court. But in these movies we are on a domestic scale and the representations are appropriately modest.

In outline, the prototypical plot is:

ORDER
   1. Introduction of the intact social group

DISORDER
   2. Disruption of the group because of (a) unjust persecution, (b) false information, (c) false accusation, or (d) prejudice (social or ethnic)
   3. Separation of the family
   4. Search for the missing member

ORDER RESTORED
   5. Reunion (on deathbed or sickbed)
   6. Final freeze frame: the group reunited

Disorder is introduced by a character we can call the "agent of disorder" who later is transformed by a sudden conversion, is never punished, and joins in the final group freeze-frame portrait.

The plot is most characteristic, and most completely worked out, in films of the Sentimental genre, where it is usually but not always a love story about a girl and a boy. But once this plot has been recognized, we begin to spot it in more fragmentary form in many other genres. This is the most Indonesian plot, for it embodies the Indonesian values of both variables noted earlier: It is concerned with people as members of the group, and it emphasizes order and disorder at the expense of good and evil.

An example of this plot is the 1982 film *Buah Hati Mama* (Mama's Sweetheart): The family—Hendrick, Nona, and their three children—has returned to Jakarta after living for years in the Netherlands. Hendrick encourages their love of Indonesia by singing sentimental songs and taking them on picnics and excursions around the Javanese countryside. But Nona is unhappy with Indonesia and particularly with Eka, their second child. Although we know that Eka is actually well behaved, he is blamed for everything that goes amiss and is beaten by Nona. Finally he runs away. They search for him. Nona, in a flash of enlightenment, realizes her faults and suddenly is at peace with Indonesia and with Eka. They find Eka near death. At the hospital, after a narrow escape, he recovers.

No single movie embodies the perfect prototype. Here there are several interesting twists to the basic plot: Nona is both the mother of the family and the agent of disorder—a combination of opposing demands which complicates her character. Her conversion brings the two sides of her character into harmony. Just as there is usually a readily recognizable agent of disorder, so there is usually one person who takes the lead in restoring order. In *Buah Hati Mama* the primary agent of order is the youngest member of the family, Putri, a girl of about six. And Putri acts as a very typical Indonesian mediator. It is through Putri that all the information necessary to reunion is passed: Putri explains to her mother that Eka did not break the new TV set; Putri tells Eka that their parents know the truth; Putri goes off holding hands with both Eka and Indra, their older brother who is the real culprit; it is Putri whom Eka, after his flight, visits surreptitiously; it is Putri who tells the family that Eka is alive; and in the hospital scene, when Eka in his delirium has a very Muslim dream about crossing a bridge to the beckoning angels, it is Putri who calls him back to the family and to life.

The basic elements of the prototype are present: false accusation, separation, search, reunion at the sickbed. In the final freeze frame of the film we see all five family members plus the little orphan boy who befriended Eka and is now presumably to be incorporated into the family. If we look at the entire range of films which use this plot frame, we see that there is a particularly great degree of variation in the triggering event—the false accusation. Some specific examples:

Someone is falsely accused of theft *(Arie Hanggara, Nila Digaun Putih)*.

A man is accused of being a Dutch spy *(Doea Tanda Mata)*.

A woman believes that she killed her best friend *(Perempuan Dalam Pasungan)*.

A woman is blamed for not being a virgin after her hymen is ruptured in a bicycle accident *(Tirai Malam Pengantin)* or when she was actually raped by a were-crocodile *(Buaya Putih)*.

A woman believes that her husband is having an affair *(Perempuan Dalam Pasungan)*.

A man blames his wife for not having revealed her mastectomy before they were married *(Akibat Kanker Payudara)*.

The false accusation can be the result of false information: She has diabetes, misunderstands a conversation and thinks her fiancé also has the disease, and she breaks off her engagement *(Badai Pasti Berlalu)*. Often the young couple is separated as a result of class prejudice where his family is superior *(Kerinduan)* or her family is superior *(Serpihan Mutiara Retak, Di Balik Kelambu)*, or where there is racial prejudice against Chinese *(Putri Giok)* or Japanese *(Bukan Sandiwara)*. It is the false accusation which gives the particular spin to the particular plot. Here the ingenuity of the scriptwriter comes into play. The other features are more or less set pieces: One member of the family flees or is driven out, suffers in a poor and miserable condition, but is finally reunited with the family.

Punishment, so necessary when Western plots work out problems of evil, is absent. The only real punishment is inflicted by parents on children, as disciplinary beatings, and usually as the result of false accusations. When someone does die at the end of a film they are killed off by the demands of the plot. They are not the guilty; in fact they are often the wronged, who must be removed to allow a harmonious family reunion. In *Ayu Dan Ayu,* for example, the man has two daughters by his wife but desperately wants a son. He seduces a Balinese dancer and they have a son. The final scene takes place at the dancer's deathbed where man, wife, and the two daughters incorporate the little boy into their family over the corpse of his mother. Family order is restored and they will live happily ever after. From a Western standpoint this is quite an extraordinary outcome. The man, an unsympathetic philandering scoundrel, achieves his wish while the dancer, victimized throughout, is painfully dispatched. (Incidentally, she is played by a leading actress who has top billing in the film.)

Even in a much more nonformulaic, auteur-type film this classic Indonesian plot can be discerned: in Teguh Karya's *Doea Tanda Mata,* Goenadi becomes a member of the group of nationalists who run the clandestine printing press in the theater and meet to discuss revolution. When his friend Asep is shot down, Goenadi is blamed and he leaves the group and loses contact with Miss Ining, a singer. There is a long search, and he finally rediscovers Miss Ining, who helps him kill the Dutch officer who shot Asep. But that same evening, another nationalist is killed by the Dutch and the group is convinced that Goenadi is actually a Dutch spy. He meets up with the group, but they kill him. Now, one might object that one cannot have it both ways. *Doea Tanda Mata* is a strongly individualistic creation of Teguh, who was both director and co-writer. But Teguh has added intertitles (in themselves a most unusual device in Indonesian cinema) to segment the plot. They read:

Semangat (enthusiasm)
Perpisahan (parting, discord)
Kehilangan Jejak (losing the trail)
Pertemuan (meeting)
Tanda Mata (keepsakes, mementos)

The film itself is an extremely effective evocation of the 1930s, and the intertitles enhance the tone by evoking in their form the silent film titles and in their content the formulaic Indonesian genre plot.

This, then, is the Indonesian plot par excellence. We have no statistics to prove that it is the most common Indonesian plot. But it is the most characteristically Indonesian in its reliance on Indo-

nesian cultural principles. And it is the most surprising for Westerners, who come to the end of the story expecting one sort of resolution and find another which makes no sense if judged by Western cultural principles. The "Indonesian plot" is not unknown in
the West, however. While thinking about this chapter I happened
to attend a performance of *As You Like It,* Shakespeare's comedy,
which is usually dated at 1600. By the final curtain I was feeling on
quite familiar ground. Not only is the plot of this play very Indonesian, but its critical reception in the West suggests some cultural
uneasiness.

As You Like It has a double plot line. Duke Senior, whose
throne has been usurped by his brother Duke Frederick, wanders
the Forest of Arden in exile. Another family has also been disrupted. Orlando, son of a deceased friend of Duke Frederick, has
been cheated out of his inheritance and is nearly killed by the
machinations of his older brother Oliver, and he, too, winds up
wandering the forest. Much of the action is taken up with the love
play, in and out of disguise, of the various principals. So far so
good. It is especially the ending which seems so Indonesian. Four
couples are finally united, but neither Duke Frederick nor Oliver
suffers. Their misdeeds are really quite considerable, but each has
had a sudden conversion. Indeed, that word is used for each
instance: Oliver, confessing, tells how Orlando saved him from a
serpent and then from a lioness, and he refers to "my conversion"
(IV.iii.137); and we hear that Duke Frederick, on his way to kill
Duke Senior, fell in with "an old religious man" and "was converted," restoring crown and lands to his wronged brother
(V.iv.161). Oliver appears in the final group scene and in some
productions Duke Frederick, now a hermit, scuttles across the
stage.

From an Indonesian standpoint, both Oliver and Duke Frederick have been agents of disorder. By casting out their brothers and
attempting fratricide they have disturbed the moral order. The
play begins at the courts, but most of it unfolds in the Forest of
Arden, a place outside the Social Order. Indeed, the exiles, whose
rightful places in the courts have been usurped, now by killing the
animals of the forest have brought their disorder to nature and are
themselves become "mere usurpers, tyrants, and what's worse"
(II.i.61). Order is gradually restored by the agents of order (Rosalind chief among them) and also by the sudden and barely moti-

vated conversions of the two agents of disorder. And in the end myriad social ties are restored or created: The two sets of brothers are reconciled and the two families are joined as Duke Senior's daughter Rosalind marries Orlando and Duke Frederick's daughter Celia weds Oliver.

Albert Gilman, editor of the Signet edition of *As You Like It,* has written that "from the eighteenth century on, critics often said that Shakespeare's craftsmanship in *As You Like It* is poor" (1963:xxi). There is a final little irony here. It seems that in the sources which Shakespeare drew on for the plot of his play, punishment is in fact meted out. In the fourteenth-century narrative poem *The Tale of Gamelyn,* which is the source of Thomas Lodge's novel *Rosalynde,* the Oliver character is hanged. Lodge himself adds the dukes but kills off the usurper (Gilman 1963:141, 142). So in his version, Shakespeare has made the plot more, not less, Indonesian. Moreover, *As You Like It* nicely observes the non-Aristotelian constraints which A. L. Becker has identified for the Javanese *wayang:* It is full of coincidences, and it begins in a court and moves to a forest. (At the end, the characters are preparing to return to the court.)

It is just those unusual features which we are here identifying as elements of the Indonesian plot that are most striking in *As You Like It* and cause the critics concern. And so I offer *As You Like It* as Shakespeare's Indonesian play—a drama in which the restoration of order replaces crime and punishment as the main driving force of the plot. Now, having looked at two prototypical Indonesian plot forms, we can turn to the features of narrative which characterize Indonesian films.

CHAPTER 5

NARRATIVE CONVENTIONS

We now turn from the tale itself to the ways of telling it. The narrative conventions are the familiar signs, symbols, settings, and scenes out of which so much of these genre films are constructed. The audiences are familiar with them and can readily read them. It is easy to disparage them as clichés of moviemaking, and certainly they do not reveal any special originality. But just because they are so standard, they form the common cultural base out of which movies are made. And of course in describing these narrative conventions we shall be looking especially for those which are particularly Indonesian—not only in the sense that they are Not Western, but also in the sense that they can be traced back to other aspects of Indonesian culture.

There are many sorts of narrative conventions of different degrees of subtlety, length, complexity, and explicitness. The conventions of Indonesian cinema can be conveniently grouped in a few categories.

CONVENTIONAL SCENES

Famous landscapes and cityscapes are often used in Indonesian movies: Particular beaches, volcanoes, parks, and gorges which are already familiar from calendars, currency, and postage stamps are favorite locations. Common examples are the highway winding into the mountains through the tea plantations south of Jakarta or the view across the Ngarai Sianok canyon at Bukittinggi, long pictured on the thousand-rupiah bill. Since so many films are shot in Jakarta itself, its major landmarks like the towering obelisk of the National Monument are convenient signals of location. Dutch buildings and even the Dutch square in front of the old city hall in Jakarta indicate a colonial period setting for the film.

Ethnic ceremonies—which usually means regional ceremonies—occur with great frequency. As noted earlier, the films are generalized Indonesian in language and plot. They may be set in a Javanese or a Minangkabau village, but rarely do people speak or behave in any specifically Javanese or Minangkabau manner. The great and almost jarring exceptions are ceremonies: In the middle of a film we are suddenly set down in a full-scale wedding ceremony or funeral or circumcision or seventh month of pregnancy rite or harvest ceremony where the extras seem to be genuine villagers wearing their own clothes and going through their accustomed rituals while the movie stars look like movie stars quite out of place. The ceremonies themselves seem authentic and are really ethnographic nuggets embedded in genre fictions. One could easily construct a fascinating survey of Indonesian ritual out of these sequences.

Another conventional scene announces that we are at a hospital: Nurses and doctors, sometimes accompanied by a distraught relative or lover, push a patient on a gurney along a covered breezeway (Photo 5). Many films involve infirmity, especially the Sentimental genre films where the denouement usually takes place around a hospital bed. So the merest glimpse of the speeding gurney and the pillared breezeway instantly communicates the setting.

CONVENTIONAL SIGNS

Conventional signs convey specific information about a character. When a young woman vomits, for instance, we know that she is pregnant. This is such a powerful sign that vomiting is not used elsewhere, by other sorts of people, to indicate, for example, drunkenness or sickness. And it usually indicates an illegitimate pregnancy—for example, when Juleha is pregnant by the were-crocodile in *Buaya Putih* (The White Crocodile). Although the audience immediately reads vomiting as a sign of pregnancy, the other characters in the film never do—apparently even the woman herself remains ignorant. And it is such a well-established sign of pregnancy that in *Galau Remaja di SMA* (Mixed-Up High School

Kids), Meriam Bellina uses vomiting as an intentional emblem to frighten her parents by pretending pregnancy.

Alcoholic beverages are widely advertised, sold, and consumed in Indonesia despite its position as the nation with the largest Muslim population in the world. But even though many Indonesians—even nominal Muslims—drink liquor, there is no aura of normalcy and glamour about drinking as there certainly is in Western cinema. Beer is usually shown in tall liter bottles, although one can rarely tell whether the brand is Bintang or Anker. Whiskey bottles, on the other hand, are readily identifiable as Johnny Walker Red. More rarely, in nightclub scenes, mixed drinks are present without an identifying bottle.

Virtually without exception, drinking signifies a weak or coarse character. The prototypical drinkers are Dutch soldiers and officers guzzling beer or sipping genever. In *Mereka Kembali* (They Return) the Dutch officer even pours beer over the head of the Republican soldiers he is interrogating. When the village headman not only betrays a prisoner to the Dutch but is patted on the head by the Dutchman's left hand and drinks beer (straight from a bottle), we understand that he has sunk to the moral depths. Corrie, the French-Indonesian girl in *Salah Asuhan* (Wrong Upbringing), drinks heavily in her apartment in Jakarta and also wears a very short minidress. When Hanafi leaves his wife to come to her, we understand that she does not (yet) have the strength of character to reject him. And of course Hanafi himself, the confused Minangkabau enamored of things Western, joins her in drinking.

In *Samiun Dan Dasima* the Englishman Eduard and his pals get drunk and have sexual orgies (albeit very tame ones) at Eduard's house in front of Dasima, the Sundanese woman who is Eduard's mistress and the mother of their child Nancy. Although Dasima is a *nyai* (a European's mistress) and although she is not a faithful Muslim, she is basically a decent woman and is repelled by the drunken carryings-on. In *Desa Di Kaki Bukit* (The Village at the Foot of the Hills) the scoundrelly clown Usman stalks into a village coffee shop, orders an empty beer bottle filled with water, and pretends to drink beer. His coarseness is all bluster, though, and he stops short of drinking real beer.

The bottles mean drinking, drinking means drunkenness, and drunkenness means confusion. Whereas order is a prime Indonesian desideratum, its opposite, confusion, is to be avoided at all costs, even as an adventure. Slowly circling merry-go-rounds exist in Indonesia, but it is hard to imagine a real roller coaster ever being a success there. The great lexical elaboration of the emotions of confusion in Minangkabau and in Indonesian indicate how salient the subject is.

Cigarettes (as well as cigars and pipes) have connotations similar to liquor but for different reasons. Tobacco is an important export crop in Indonesia; Muslim males are not forbidden to smoke (except during daylight hours in the fasting month); and even the strong clove-flavored cigarettes do not bring on dizziness. But generally the same weak or coarse or disorderly men who drink also smoke. And the admirable men do not. Karimun, the wise older man in *Desa Di Kaki Bukit* does smoke a pipe, but the village is, after all, a center of tobacco cultivation and so Karimun's smoking does not seem out of character. A more typical pipe smoker is the weak father in *Mereka Kembali* (They Return) in the early part of the film when he is still pandering to the Dutch officers and before his wife and daughters have shamed him into aiding the revolution.

So, although tobacco signifies much the same as liquor in these films, we are hard put to explain it. Chewing betel, on the other hand, is done exclusively by women (who almost never smoke or drink) and then by older village women. As we shall see in the next chapter, it is a sign of extreme traditional Indonesian-ness. In her later years the actress Fifi Young practically owned the old village woman's roles, and her trademark was a great chaw of betel. In *Salah Asuhan* she hunkers down on the floor and chews betel, driving her westernized son Hanafi to distraction.

The usual sign of a woman's insanity is her long loose hair. Indonesian women in general take great pains with their coiffeurs. Traditional women, and most women in formal or traditional settings, put up their hair, often building it into a chignon around a false hairpiece. The disorder of long loose-hanging hair is thus particularly striking and may have various meanings. When Fitri goes mad with remorse in *Perempuan Dalam Pasungan* (The Woman in Stocks) she lets her hair go loose (Photo 6). The deranged old couple living in the jungle in *Buaya Putih* (The White Crocodile) both have long unkempt hair. But it can also be a sign of extreme mourning—as for Halima after the death of her young husband in *Si Doel Anak Betawi* (Doel—The Betawi Kid). In *Desa Di Kaki Bukit* (The Village at the Foot of the Hills) both Santi, the sophisticated sex bomb from Jakarta who wants to reclaim the hero, as well as The Prostitute (who never seems to actually ply her trade but is the partner of Usman of the water-filled beer bottle), sport loose hair. But all the various examples of careless hair have a common underlying meaning—disorder, whether it is the mental disorder of madness, the moral disorder of unbound sexuality, or the emotional disorder of grief.

At the opposite extreme, we can note two extraordinary uses of stocks—the wooden frame for public punishment—as a sign of order restored. In both cases a young woman sits on the floor of a back room, her legs straight in front of her, locked into wooden stocks, her hair wild and loose. And in each case she has been put into the stocks by her father for violations of order beyond tolera-tion. In the horror film *Buaya Putih* (The White Crocodile) Juleha is pregnant by a magical were-crocodile who raped her. Her father thinks that her sin was merely extramarital disorder. We know that, however involuntary it was on Juleha's part, the act was much worse: It was extraspecies disorder. In the sentimental film *Perempuan Dalam Pasungan* (The Woman in Stocks), Fitria is driven to a state of confusion and jealousy when her college room-mate (her husband's former girlfriend) shows up at their house in Jakarta. Her confusion feeds on itself until she comes to believe that she is the cause of her friend's death. She finally goes mad and her father takes her home to Yogyakarta where he hides her away from the world and her family in the back room—in stocks. And stocks, which hold the legs straight, parallel, and immobile, are the ultimate physical manifestation of imposed order.

"BANANA PEEL" SIGNS

Certain narrative conventions can be called "banana peel" signs—premonitory devices which predict a future event. If in an Ameri-can comedy or cartoon the camera picks up a banana peel tossed in someone's path, we know with certainty what will happen next: Someone will step on the banana peel and do a silly pratfall. We anticipate not only the event (the fall) but also its connotation (funny).

In Indonesian films scissors presage stabbing. There is no obvi-ous cultural reason for this association, but it is a regular conven-tion. If the camera isolates a pair of scissors, we know it will be used as a weapon. This is an Indonesian variation on Chekov's famous dictum: If you introduce a pistol in the first act of a play you must use it by the third act. There is a sort of meta-reference to the convention in *Akibat Kanker Payudara* (Because of Breast Cancer) where the girl, distraught, looks meaningfully at the scissors and then her parents step in, making her promise not to use them on herself. I realized the strength of this Indonesian convention when Teguh Karya, a master of filmmaking, violated it in *Badai Pasti Berlalu* (The Storm Is Finally Past). The camera picked up a pair of scissors but never referred to them again and I realized that I was left with a feeling of unresolved tension: What happened with the scissors?

A second banana peel sign is a young woman bathing in a stream, usually a pool at the foot of a waterfall. She walks away from the camera into the pool, strips to the waist, still with her back to the camera, and begins to bathe. She thinks she is alone but the audience knows that this idyllic scene will quickly turn into one of danger. She will discover a peeping tom who will attempt to rape her. In the West the biblical story of Susanna and the Elders provided the excuse for a whole genre of erotic guilt art. (Look! Aren't those men horrible!) In Indonesian films this conventional situation is one of the few justifiable circumstances for showing a woman's body (albeit little more than her upper back) and, like virtually all such peeks, it ends in sexual violence.

A quite common premonitory sign is the breaking of glass, which anticipates some sort of disaster. It may be blatantly handled, as in *Si Doel Anak Betawi:* The father is arguing with the mother and in his annoyance he hits the wall, knocking down his framed portrait. The glass breaks and now there are several quick close-ups cutting back and forth to him, horrified, and to her, anxious, and to the broken glass, as the music swells and threatens. A couple of scenes later he dies. In this film both actors and audience are fully aware of the heavy-handed implications of the broken glass. It only stops short of having a subtitle reading "Disaster to Follow." Usually the broken glass event is more subtle—say, someone accidentally knocks a glass off a table. The camera may emphasize the act, but the players themselves show no recognition of the meaning of the sign.

PARALINGUISTIC SIGNS

There is a puzzling paralinguistic feature—a little explosive sigh usually done by women at the beginning of a conversation where they are for some reason uneasy—that is very common in Indonesian movies. It may well be an accurately reported feature of Indonesian talk. The nature of movies, which allow one to be an uninvolved but close-up observer of the intense emotions of others, may make this act especially obvious. In the rare instances when I was comparably close to real-life intense emotion in Indonesia I was not an effectively distant sociolinguist.

This explosive sigh occurs, for example, in *Samiun Dan Dasima* when Samiun and Dasima have their first arranged meeting leading to their affair—Dasima shows her self-conscious awareness of the situation by the sigh. Later, after their first night together, she does the little sigh as he quickly and coolly dresses and leaves. At the end, when Dasima is saying goodbye to the old servant whom she trusts (but who has actually betrayed her), they hug and in her sadness Dasima does the sigh. Although men rarely do it, Samiun does the sign in a couple of his tense/nervous/guilty/angry encounters with the Chinese moneylenders. Future study may reveal whether the explosive sigh is really a theatrical sign or simply a feature of Indonesian conversation.

THE ANGER FACE

The ambivalent status of anger is obvious: Anger is dangerous, controlled, but also fascinating. This is true generally, but especially so for Indonesians. Viewing intense anger in film is a way of experiencing the forbidden. But we find an even more striking example of the working out of this ambivalence when we look at the facial expressions for anger which appear in Indonesian films.

Recent research on the emotions has demonstrated that not only are a few facial expressions for emotions recognized panculturally, but these faces have psychophysiological consequences which are found in all humans. The anger face, for example, involves certain facial muscle groups. When these muscle groups are contracted, the pancultural anger face results (Photo 7): brows down and together, upper eyelids raised, lower eyelids tensed, lips compressed or parted to reveal clenched teeth (see Ekman and Friesen 1975:78–98). Further, when all the anger face muscle groups are activated, the autonomic nervous system reacts with a set of anger-specific changes—and, also, people report that they *feel* angry. It appears that there are "hard-wired" connections between facial muscles, the autonomic nervous system, and the cognitive areas of the brain. This means, for example, that there is built into the human body the potential, at least, for a continuously escalating spiral of anger: Making the anger face results in a feeling of anger, which results in a more intense anger face, and so on (see Ekman, Levenson, and Friesen 1983).

Thus it seems that the basic human biology constitutes a system in which anger can easily intensify. But what of Indonesia, a culture area in which anger is so controlled and suppressed? The answer seems to be that Indonesia has an anger face which is not an anger face. That is to say, there is a facial expression which is readily recognizable as "anger" but in which the eyebrows are raised high—not lowered as they should be in the pancultural anger expression (Photo 8). Remember that the autonomic nervous system's feedback loop only works when all the muscle groups for the anger face are in play. Raising the eyebrows takes a different set of muscles from those used for lowering the eyebrows. Thus, the brows-raised anger face is a cultural emblem for anger but does not run the risk of setting up the anger-intensifying feedback loop. So Indonesian culture has bypassed biology.

In ordinary life, of course, one has little opportunity to observe intense anger. And when one is actually in an anger situation one is rarely an effective observer anyway. I first came across the anger emblem when my anthropology students at Andalas University in West Sumatra collected lists of emblems from Minangkabau informants. One year they did it in the Minangkabau language and one year in Indonesian. Most of the emblems were hand gestures of one sort of another, but this brows-raised anger face appeared in both the Minangkabau and the Indonesian language collections. Thus alerted, I turned back to the Indonesian movies. There, roughly half of the strong anger expressions were brows down and half were brows up. Anger in movies—done with lowered brows or especially done with raised brows—turns out to be a safe way for Indonesians to enjoy the forbidden sensation of extreme anger.

SEXUALITY

Sexuality is one of the most sensitive subjects of Indonesian life. Most films try to deal with it in some way or another, yet there are inherent problems particular to Indonesian filmmakers. Although the norms which govern sexuality are strong and keenly held, the different cultures of Indonesia have sexual norms which in some details at least are quite different and even mutually incompatible. While films do avoid the regional language barriers by using the national language, there is no comparable solution available for sexuality. And to further complicate the filmmakers' lives, their Indonesian films are held to stricter standards by the censorship board than are foreign films shown in the same movie theaters. So the filmgoing public in Indonesia can have access to scenes of sexual explicitness in foreign films which would be quite impossible in Indonesian films. The filmmaker must therefore satisfy a wide variety of desires and expectations while not offending another range of contradictory norms.

Given the impossibility of these demands it is no wonder that an elaborate pattern of narrative conventions has been developed to allude to sexuality without actually presenting it. And of course these patterns, or visual euphemisms, change as the culture changes. Here we shall explore those narrative conventions dealing with sexuality which have been used in the recent past, while at the same time anticipating that in a decade or so they will seem quaint and outmoded. In Western cinema there was once a convention of tilting the camera up—away from the embracing couple toward the ceiling or the mantlepiece or the clouds—to indicate that serious hanky-panky was now taking place just offscreen. Today such a shot would get only derisive laughter from an American audience. Some of these Indonesian conventions, which are more poetic, like breaking glass to presage disaster, will probably persist. But most of the euphemistic conventions are likely to change.

Until very recently, sexuality in Indonesian movies has either been downplayed or presented as sadism. Sex itself is rape: In the Japanese Period films, Japanese soldiers are shown raping Indonesian women. The scenes are visually explicit. In *Kadarwati* the naked breasts of the women were obscured by a printing technique of burning out the center of the frames. Sexual intercourse is also suggested fairly explicitly in Horror genre films—as in *Buaya Putih,* when Juleha is being raped by the were-crocodile, or when her daughter lures the motorcycle gang into the bushes for serial sex and then turns into a crocodile. This second scene, which begins as horror, turns comical as the obese motorcyclist realizes that he is engaging a crocodile, not a woman.

But in those films where sex may fairly be considered an act of love and tenderness, it takes place far offscreen. Even the conventional depiction of childbirth stages it as rape. Indeed, the camera takes the point of view of the male violator: The woman is on her back, moaning and writhing in agony, the camera on a tripod between her legs shooting down on her face. (Childbirth is made so explicit and horrible in these films that it is a wonder Indonesian women dare to have children at all.)

Kissing—full lip-to-lip kisses—was only rarely shown in Indonesian movies until very recently. The convention was to film the complete kiss and then in editing to cut the shot at the last frame before actual lip contact was made. So technically the couple does not kiss on screen. There is at least one early exception to this convention: In *Cintaku Di Kampus Biru* (My Love on the Blue Campus, 1977), there is a full lip kiss. But it was only in the late 1980s that kissing became common.

Palm-to-palm hand holding is even more taboo than kissing. Although a courting couple, for example, may touch hands, it is always palm to back of hand. If walking together down the street, the boy holds the girl's wrist or they lock fingers. But palms never touch. Sometimes the staging is such that it is very difficult for the actor and actress not to touch palms. In *Buaya Putih,* for instance, as Firman and Nurbiah are walking through the woods he helps her over a large log and their hands have to do a complicated little dance of avoidance. In *Desa Di Kaki Bukit,* when Wati and Rais finally come together, she is holding a pinecone and his hand caresses the pinecone and her hand but somehow manages not to make palm contact (Photo 9). In *Buaya Putih* again, when Nurbiah (who is actually a were-crocodile) attacks Firman on their honeymoon, they make full palm-to-palm contact with both hands as he tries to ward her off. But this is a scene of extreme horror and the violation of the palm-to-palm taboo serves to intensify the atmosphere.

By the late 1980s this rule began to break down, but much more

slowly than the prohibition against full kissing. One of the earliest
violations is instructive. First of all, it occurs in *Carok* (Duel), a
film set in Madura. The boy and girl, after coffee at a dockside
cafe, walk away hand in hand, palm to palm. But these two are
not proper Javanese. They are not even the relatively proper
Minangkabau. They are Madurese, who have a reputation for
extreme coarseness and violence and, who knows, probably have
been holding hands like this for generations. The camera work is
nice: We see the girl and boy in full bodies from a distance and
then the camera cuts in to a close-up of their palm-to-palm hands
—as if to emphasize just how extraordinary this event is. Another
early example is in *Cintaku Di Kampus Biru,* but here, again, the
boy at least is from Menado, a westernized Christian region of
Sulawesi. The rule even seems to hold in situations unrelated to
courtship: When Hanafi is reunited briefly with Corrie at her
deathbed in *Salah Asuhan,* he tenderly holds her hand, begging
forgiveness, but even then they do not make palm-to-palm contact
(Photo 10).

The palm-to-palm contact avoidance rule strikes the Western
viewer as somewhat exotic. That kissing should be prohibited is no
surprise, since it was also taboo in Western cinema in the 1930s for
the same reasons. But Western conventions are neutral about
palm-to-palm contact. In fact, for most Indonesians this rule is
not even explicit, even though the visual evidence makes it clear
just how strong the taboo is. The reason for the rule is rooted in
the impurity of the left hand. In Indonesia, as generally throughout Asia, the left hand is specifically marked as impure. This is not
merely a part of the abstract symbol system. Since the left hand is
used with water to clean oneself after defecation, it is physically
impure as well. Those whose cultures are relatively indifferent to
the left hand (and especially those of us who are actually left-
handed) must exercise great discipline when traveling in Asia. To
use the left hand in giving or receiving objects, in touching
another, or in putting food to the mouth can give great offense,
for such use of the left hand says, symbolically, "shit!"

Now, when two people walk side by side the right hand of one is
next to the (impure) left hand of the other. It is contaminating
enough to touch left hand to right. But to clasp the left palm to the
other's right palm is out of the question. And although the rule is
less explicit for Indonesians than the rule against kissing—the one

is mentioned in the Censorship Code, the other is not—it seems more robust and is changing more slowly.

Two major sources of inspiration for the visual arts of Indonesia are the West and India. In both, the female body is presented as an object of beauty and eroticism. But this aspect of Indonesian arts, at least, is firmly Islamicized. In Indonesian cinema women's bodies are generally fully draped in shapeless clothing. The focus is on the face, not the body. This convention is changing in films only slowly, like the kissing convention. There are exceptions, however, in the sadistic/erotic displays of bodies in Japanese Period and Horror genre films. The Western-style eroticism seems to be coming into Indonesian cinema via the High School genre films where more and more frequently the girls wear tight and scanty clothing.

Red blouses seem to be a very special emblem of sexuality. In *Perempuan Dalam Pasungan* (The Woman in Stocks) it is made quite explicit when the busybody neighbor warns Fitria to watch out since her friend rode off with Andi, her husband, wearing a red blouse and we know that means she is making a pass at him. Actually, years before, Fitria had worn her friend's red blouse (presumably not the same blouse) when she went on a date with Andi that resulted in their marriage. In *Si Doel Anak Betawi,* the young widow wears a red blouse when she goes with Asmat, her brother-in-law, to the grave of Asman, her husband, and the outcome is that Asmat woos her and proposes marriage. In *Samiun Dan Dasima,* Dasima wears a red blouse for her assignation with Samiun which results in their living together. In all four cases, the woman wearing red is quite a decent person, not at all a vamp (despite the accusation of the nosy neighbor).

OTHER ASPECTS OF CONVENTION

There are certainly many other Indonesian-specific narrative conventions which I have missed or do not understand. Heavy rain, for example, especially when the camera zooms up close to show it running off a roof or gushing across a road, often seems to be followed immediately by some disaster. A systematic study of the camera conventions would probably turn up some Indonesian ways of framing, cutting, or juxtapositioning scenes. A rapid, almost disorienting, zoom in and out on a subject occurs frequently in comedies, for example, and in comic scenes of other films. We have already noted the generally negative connotations of disorientation or dizziness of any sort in Indonesia, but here it is used for humorous effect.

These narrative conventions are the building blocks of Indonesian movie plots. Like the (Indonesian) language and the (Indonesian) players, clothing, and scenery, they are what the filmmakers have on hand. As they are conventions, they turn up especially in conventional, or genre, films. In Teguh Karya's *Doea Tanda Mata,* which is certainly an individualistic, auteur film, one finds virtually none of these conventions. Just as the auteur films have plots which are relatively unique or nonformulaic, so they also tend to avoid, consciously or unconsciously, these narrative conventions.

CHAPTER 6

MODELS FOR MODERNIZATION

So far we have considered the thesis that the cinema of a culture, like any other significant product of that culture, must embody to some degree its basic patterns. (See, for example, Kracauer's 1947 treatment of German film, Wolfenstein and Leites' 1950 treatment of American, English, and French films, and Mellen's 1976 treatment of Japanese films.) This has been a useful guiding principle for research but it hardly counts as an important discovery.

Yet the idea that cinema is an active agent of change is a much more controversial notion, at least for social scientists. James Peacock's study of *ludruk,* the lower-class folk drama in East Java, is the prototype for treating such theater as a "rite of modernization." From this perspective, *ludruk* offers role models for modernization to its proletarian audiences. Peacock has discussed (in the 1987 afterword to his 1968 classic) how critics of his study expressed reservations about his strategy of looking at the function of *ludruk* as an agent of change—or, at least, a facilitator and stimulus to individuals to undertake modernization. Indeed, it is more common these days to treat theater and ritual in terms of structure and symbolism. But the success of Peacock's study demonstrates the usefulness of examining the ways in which a performance genre functions in the larger cultural context. (Although Ward Keeler's 1987 book on *wayang* and the chapter in James Siegel's 1986 book on the city of Solo, treating the *Sri Mulat* theater, focus on other problems, they do not totally ignore the functions of these theatrical genres.)

In the world outside academia, however, the common wisdom holds that films and video are powerful shapers of behavior. The advertising income of television not only drives the content of pro-

grams on television, it dictates the scheduling of the World Series
and Winter Olympics. And the wealth or poverty of television
advertising budgets makes or breaks presidential campaigns—all
this in the firm belief that those little films which we call ads can in
fact influence a nation's buying patterns or voting behavior.

On the American political scene, likewise, since the 1930s the
film industry has been subject to—perhaps captive of—various
interests who want to control what is shown on the screen. This
censorship, whether self-imposed or applied from the outside, has
two themes. One is that certain subjects are offensive to parts of
the population and on that account should not be seen by anyone.
The other theme is more interesting for our purposes: It is the firm
belief that people's behavior will be altered by what they see on the
screen—that viewing sexual acts ("pornography") will lead viewers to imitate those acts, that viewing violence will encourage viewers to commit similar acts of violence, and that viewing political
acts depicted in a favorable (or unfavorable) light will create in
viewers a favorable (or unfavorable) attitude toward that political
position ("propaganda"). Indeed in the heyday of American political censorship, the 1940s, both the Communist Party of America
and the House Committee were convinced that touches of "Communist Propaganda" inserted surreptitiously into films would
convert the American people to communism—and both parties
acted accordingly. The accuracy of these beliefs is in question.
Indeed, much research has been done on the question of violence
and the media, and it is still a matter of debate to what degree
viewing filmed violence actually decreases violence through ca-
tharsis or increases it through stimulation. In place of solid information, we are left with a few anecdotal horror stories.

A NEW APPROACH TO CHARACTER TYPES

The purpose of this chapter is to assume both Peacock's thesis and
his strategy—that genres of popular culture do offer models for
character and behavior which people may use for guidance or
inspiration to move in unfamiliar directions and that it is worth-
while to push this thesis as far as possible to learn something new
about how these genres work. In the case of *ludruk,* Peacock
found Javanese who were quite explicitly aware of the modernizing functions of the performances. I do not want to claim too

much for Indonesian cinema at this point, although Indonesian film people I have spoken to clearly express a sense of mission, a feeling that their films promote a better society.

In some cases, Indonesian films quite straightforwardly present the case for cultural change of one sort or another. *Putri Giok* (The Jade Princess) is about interethnic relationships. In this case, the issue is tensions between Indonesians and Chinese—or, more precisely, between people who, although they may have lived in Indonesia for generations, are still racially and culturally somewhat distinct and recognizable as Chinese and, on the other hand, the "native" Indonesians, racially and culturally identified as one of the older populations of the archipelago. Chinese immigration was encouraged by the Dutch during the colonial period, and the Dutch gave these Chinese considerable economic power to offset the political power of the majority groups already living in the archipelago. The Chinese Indonesians have long posed a problem for the republic: They are perceived as at once essential to the economic life and a threat to the political life of the country. They are subjected to special restrictions and are even, on occasion, the special focus of pogroms. In fact, in Indonesian movies it is rare to see Chinese characters at all, except in minor comic roles.

But in *Putri Giok* the teenage brother and sister of a Chinese-Indonesian family are dating a girl and a boy of Indonesian families. The Chinese father intervenes, the relationships are broken off, the youths suffer, and the film concludes didactically with two optional endings. In the first, one couple commits suicide in despair and the families face each other at grave side; in the second, the families see the light, the couple are reunited in the spirit of Pancasila, the Five Principles of the Republic, and everyone is uplifted in patriotic fervor.

In *Desa Di Kaki Bukit* (The Village at the Foot of the Hills) the isolation of a Javanese village is ended by a new bridge which brings in a new schoolteacher, a nurse, and various Jakarta lowlife characters. The conservative elements of the village resist the school and the family planning clinic until each dramatically proves its worth, and then the entire village embraces change.

On the most obvious level, these two films are examples of plots which celebrate modernization: They map the triumph of the modern and the defects of the traditional ethnic or village isolation. But on this same surface level, many films seem to be saying the opposite: The most modern figures are shown as totally corrupt, and the village, not the city, is the source of virtue. The way out of this paradox is to locate the various characters not in terms of a single dimension (traditional to modern) but in terms of two cross-cutting axes: Traditional/Modern and Indonesian/Western.

Those familiar with Peacock's analysis of *ludruk* will note a similarity: He uses the opposing pairs traditional/modern and also the opposing pairs refined/coarse. He finds that the first opposition is a concern in the traditional village setting, where lower, coarser, classes are in conflict with upper, more refined, classes. In *ludruk* plots set in more modern contexts, the concern has shifted from class opposition to progressive/reactionary or traditional/modern opposition. Thus jokes in the first plot type hinge on the coarse/refined opposition, while jokes in the modern plot type tend to be concerned with traditional/modern opposition.

Here, however, I want to introduce a grid to represent characters. The grid is constructed with the two axes—Traditional/Modern and Indonesian/Western—and is intended to make sense of what is going on in the films. The choice of these particular axes is one way of making explicit a basic concern of many Indonesians: It is often phrased in terms of modernizing without losing the national identity or in terms of acquiring the West's good features while avoiding its corruption. There are various ways of formulating the problem. In his essay on the 1940 novel *Belenggu (Shackles)*, William H. Frederick mentioned that much Western criticism has interpreted the novel in terms of the "straightforward dichotomies" of "East and West, tradition and modernity" (1985:12). Benedict Anderson (1978) has shown how postrevolutionary monument building in Indonesia has strongly reaffirmed ties with the past, and he discusses how contemporary political cartoons completely ignore the presence of foreigners. Harsya Bachtiar (1985) has discussed contemporary Indonesia in terms of agreement and conflict between four different cultural systems: regional ethnic, major religious, national, and foreign. But when we look specifically at Indonesian movies, we see that regional cultures and religions, Bachtiar's first two systems, do not come into play except as background settings. It is the third and fourth systems which provide the conflict in these films. There are certainly different ways to construct this sort of analytical framework, but these two axes—Indonesian/Western and Traditional/Modern—turn out to be especially revealing.

The two axes give us four types of characters to examine in

terms of modernization. (This is not to claim, of course, that films are written, cast, or criticized in terms of these four categories. They are an order imposed from without. The test of their usefulness is the strength they give to the analysis.) Before looking at particular films, however, let us look at the four character types.

Modern-Western: In Indonesian films, most Europeans and a few Indonesians fit this category. They are urban and have lived in Jakarta or Europe. They wear European-style clothing which violates Indonesian standards of propriety: Women usually wear miniskirts and sleeveless blouses. (But it should be pointed out that even these costumes are not particularly form-revealing by the standards of the Western films seen in Indonesia.) Drinking beer, wine, or hard liquor is a standard act of these people and rarely if ever done by anyone else. They show little respect for traditional aspects of Indonesian life. They may be central or peripheral to the plot, but by the time of the denouement they have either been transformed into Modern-Indonesian types or have simply been discarded. (They die, move back to Jakarta, etc.)

Modern-Indonesian: These are the admired people in Indonesian films. This is the quadrant of the grid toward which movement takes place. They are always Indonesians, usually young or middle-aged. If male, they probably wear Western-style dress, but if female they usually wear traditional Indonesian dress—the wrapped batik-pattern sarong skirt and the loose, long-sleeved kebaya blouse. They never smoke and they never drink alcohol.

The Kartini figure in the Kartini corner of the grid is a special subset of this general type. Ibu Kartini (Ibu means mother, Mrs., Ma'am—a term used to indicate respect for an older woman) has emerged as one of the key icons in popular Indonesian thinking (Taylor 1976, 1989). The actual Kartini was the daughter of a Javanese nobleman. She lived at the turn of the century, got an excellent Dutch education, and is best known in the West for her letters to her Dutch friends, some of which have been published. She was a strong feminist and nationalist. Ibu Kartini Day is one of the few national holidays which is not religious. Kartini herself did marry at the age of twenty-four and died a year later in childbirth. But she is now celebrated not so much as a feminist but rather as the role model for the modern, yet very Indonesian, woman. And although she was only twenty-five when she died, her image today is that of the middle-aged matron. Certainly her usual title, Ibu, reinforces that image.

In many Indonesian movies there is one figure, a woman, usually middle-aged, always dressed in elegant Indonesian attire, her face the prototype of Indonesian feminine beauty, who is a minor character but whose role in the film at a certain moment is crucial. She intervenes, offers good advice, and is important as an agent who restores order. The salience of the order/disorder theme in Indonesian movies cannot be overemphasized. As I suggested in Chapter 3, struggles are not so much between good guys and bad guys as between order and disorder: Someone causes disorder, and others eventually restore order. The Kartini figure is the *dea ex machina* who restores order.

Traditional-Western: Almost by definition, these characters do not show up in Indonesia, or in Indonesian films, and so this quadrant is rarely occupied in the corpus of Indonesian cinema. Old DeBusse, the French botanist in *Salah Asuhan,* does fit this category, but it is significant that the plot does not really get rolling until after his death.

Traditional-Indonesian: These traditional Indonesian adults are always dressed conservatively, often chew betel recreationally (not just ceremonially), and represent the unchanging elements in the plot. They are always treated sympathetically and often move toward modernization. But they tend to be old, poor, less than attractive, even slightly comical in their old-fashioned ways. The epitome of this role was played by a famous actress, Fifi Young, in her later years. Still active until her recent death, she was the last of the prewar film stars. (Although she played the ultimate old village Ibu, she herself was of Chinese-French background.) A subtype here is a very Javanese man, dressed in very Javanese clothing, complete with batik cap with bulb hanging down the back. He is usually comical, blundering, and pompous, uses exaggerated Javanese gestures of politeness, and is rarely treated with sympathy.

Using the label "Indonesian" for the non-Western end of one axis might seem a bit problematic at first. In the actual Indonesian experience there is considerable tension between the national culture and language—"Indonesian"—and the regional cultures and languages such as Javanese, Minangkabau, and Batak. In real life the options for modernization are correspondingly more complex. But movie life does not reflect this national/regional contrast. The films are all made in the national language, Indonesian, for a nationwide audience. There is no regional film industry, even in Java. Regional languages and European languages are used for special effects, but almost never do they have to carry the major plot line. (A significant exception to this rule is *Tjoet Nya Dien*, which swept the Citra awards in 1988.) Perhaps for this reason, and because of the political sensitivity of the regionalism issue, even the films which are set in a particular (non-Javanese) region manage to gloss over regional characteristics to a great extent.

Thus in these films one hears good Indonesian spoken even in Sumatran family scenes or in Javanese villages where the regional language would certainly be spoken. Other ethnographic particulars are also generalized away. The supposedly Minangkabau setting of *Salah Asuhan* (Wrong Upbringing) is altered, for example, dropping the specifically matrilineal twists to the plot in favor of a Standard Patrilineal Indonesian situation. Since the films are often shot on location, regional landscape, architecture, and costumes may be written in. Often scenes of specific regional ceremonies, especially weddings, are cut into the films. But plots do not depend on the specifics of local culture. One could not do successful regional ethnography on the basis of the plots. Therefore, it seems justifiable to analyze the modernization in the films as Western vs. a generalized, homogenized, national "Indonesian." The complexities of regionalism are indeed real, but they are not confronted in the films.

The grid, then, gives us four ideal types. In the broader sense they represent four categories which comfortably encompass most of the characters in most Indonesian films. Now let us turn to two films where we can analyze characters and plot development in terms of this grid.

SALAH ASUHAN

Salah Asuhan (Wrong Upbringing) is a 1972 film version of the 1928 book by Abdoel Moeis. The book is perhaps the best known of all Indonesian novels and is still assigned reading in Indonesian schools. (I am not sure if it is the *Silas Marner* of Indonesia or the *Gone With the Wind* of Indonesia.) Like many Indonesian novels,

it explores the tension and contradictions between traditional customs and modern patterns. Probably because of the difficulty of
creating a 1920s setting, the movie was updated to the early 1970s.
This transposition compromised the validity of the film—Indonesians who can accept the story as set in 1928 often feel that it is
totally unreal for the postindependence era.

The title sets the tone: The young man, Hanafi, has been given a
European education and now feels himself superior to his own culture and rejects his obligations toward his own society. Hanafi's
upbringing has been wrong, even false. It has landed him at the
extreme of the Modern-Western category and he is good for nothing. (See Figure 1.) He makes fun of his old mother, who squats
around his house chewing betel. He insults even those of his ten-
nis-playing friends who have not gone to the right (that is, Western) schools. He desperately wants to marry a French-Indonesian
girl, Corrie, but when she leaves him he falls deathly ill. When he
finally recovers, he reluctantly and petulantly marries his first
cousin, Rapiah. They have a little boy, but Hanafi is never content
and finally he runs off to Jakarta, marries Corrie after all, bungles
that marriage, and after Corrie's death returns to apologize to his
mother and walks away, presumably to commit suicide.

Corrie too is Modern-Western and, however unsympathetic, is
perhaps more a victim of circumstances than really rotten. Her
Indonesian mother has died and she lives with her French father.
Her father discourages her marriage to Hanafi on the grounds that

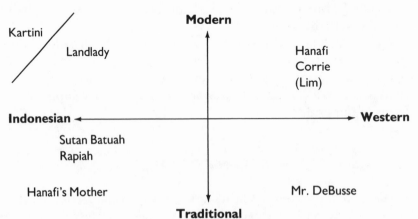

**Figure 1. The Modernization Grid: *Salah Asuhan*
(Wrong Upbringing)**

mixed marriages such as his own do not work out in the end. Interestingly, she obeys her parent (unlike Hanafi) and leaves for Jakarta. But as soon as her father has died, Hanafi comes looking for her in Jakarta and they get married. In this sense she is not quite so extreme as Hanafi, for she does listen to her family's wishes about marriage. But she has the other attributes of the Modern-Western character: She wears short, form-revealing clothes on the tennis court in town as well as in Jakarta; she has wine bottles sitting out on a table in her apartment in Jakarta; and she tells how, when she learned of her father's death, she got drunk—and then proceeds to drink with Hanafi.

Mr. DeBusse is a rare type: the Traditional-Western character. He lives quietly in the countryside hunting ducks and daily visiting the grave of his wife. He is introduced with classical Western music, and we learn that he comes from noble French stock. His one desire is that Corrie, his daughter, should return to France to reclaim the family estates and redeem his own name. He quotes Kipling when advising his daughter against marrying Hanafi: "East is East and West is West . . ."

Hanafi's mother is Traditional-Indonesian. Her personal habits are typical of the village: She chews betel, hunkers on the floor, and complains that Hanafi's house is uncomfortable, like that of a Dutchman. She understands some of the problem but not all. She seems to have supported Hanafi's modernization but not his de-Indonesianization—he certainly could not have gone to school in Holland for ten years without her approval, but on his return she insists that he honor the betrothal which she and her brother arranged for their children years before. And in the final lines of the film, she comes to some realization when she says, "All people are born good. It's only that we aren't smart enough in bringing them up." *(Semua manusia dilahirkan baik. Hanya kita juga tak pandai mengasuh.)*

Rapiah and her father, Sutan Batuah, are both Traditional-Indonesian, although not quite so extreme as Hanafi's mother. We actually know little about Sutan Batuah. He has a clan title, Sutan, which is very Indonesian (Minangkabau) but gives no clue as to his modernness. He did support Hanafi's ten-year education in Holland, but he then wanted to hold Hanafi to the arranged marriage with his daughter.

We know a bit more about Rapiah. She is a classic Indonesian beauty and wears the Indonesian clothing appropriate to the Kartini figure. There is even the suggestion that if Hanafi were to guide her, she would emerge as a truly Modern-Indonesian woman. But, owing to her ineptness with things modern, Hanafi is not willing. Although she has been to school and can read Indonesian in Latin script, she cannot manage the Western-style food which Hanafi serves nor the Western utensils with which Hanafi has set his Western table, assuring her humiliation. When he entertains his tennis friends, she breaks off her labors in the kitchen and, with her hair loose, serves tea looking like a servant and setting off Hanafi's anger: "Village women don't know how things should be ordered! You're a slob!" *(Perempuan kampung tidak tau aturan! Kurang ajar!)*

There is one true Kartini figure: Corrie's landlady in Jakarta. The landlady is a classic Indonesian beauty, matronly in her thirties, well dressed in sarong and kebaya, wearing glasses, and in complete control of the situation. When Corrie's attempts to find a job have been frustrated by false rumors that she has been a high-class prostitute, and then by an employer who is more interested in her body than her typing skill, she returns in despair to her house. The landlady meets her, commiserates, says that she believes her, and then arranges for her to get a job in Bandung in an orphanage. When Hanafi comes looking for Corrie, the landlady treats him a good deal more sympathetically than he perhaps deserves, saying that he should give Corrie some time to get over the false accusations (which we know were made by Hanafi himself among others). In this film the Kartini-landlady does try to set things in order, but she is too late: Corrie dies and Hanafi kills himself anyway. But on the analogy with other Indonesian movies, it is very clear that she is the Kartini type.

A final character in the film who is worth mentioning is Lim, an elegant Chinese procuress for wealthy Chinese men. Lim befriends Corrie in Jakarta after her marriage to Hanafi. Hanafi has gotten a good job, they live in a Western-style house, and Corrie is left alone during the day. (Corrie addresses Lim as "Tante," the Dutch word for aunt, a respectful familiar term for an older woman.) When Corrie finally realizes the implication of the gifts which Lim has been pressing on her, she throws her out. But Hanafi has already been made suspicious by Lim's visits. When he accuses Corrie of being unfaithful, she leaves. Lim is thoroughly Modern, as shown by her Western dress and her immorality. But she is so strongly identified with the Chinese men for whom she is arranging things that it is hard to call her Western. In this sense, the two-dimensional scheme falls short and we should allow for an auxiliary plane—a Chinese plane—to supplement the Western axis. That is, Lim is Modern-Chinese.

Thus are the characters of *Salah Asuhan* located in terms of the modernization grid. In fact, for both literary effect and as a model of modernization, they are located much too firmly. There is no movement, no development of character, in these terms at all. Hanafi's first, traditional, marriage to Rapiah is done out of physical weakness and with extreme ill-natured contempt. He does not budge from his Western-Modern position at all, and his final ritual abasement at his mother's feet is too late to save him. As his mother says to Rapiah, "Let him go, 'Piah, we don't need him any more. Only God can show him the way." Because of Hanafi's intransigence, Rapiah's potential for modernization is never realized.

Much could be said about the Indonesian-ness of this film. The themes of order and disorder are so strong that it could well have been called "Confused Upbringing" because of the two mixed marriages which brought so much disorder to the lives of all concerned. (The linguist Ellen Rafferty tells me that all the problems were caused by one man who was confused because of his upbringing.) Although the main characters are Minangkabau, as is the director (Asrul Sani), and the film was shot on location in West Sumatra, both geographically and ethnographically it is woefully inaccurate. The novel was a sharp criticism of the Dutch period's racial and social discrimination, much of which has disappeared in the transformation of the 1928 novel into the 1980s film. In the end, we can say that *Salah Asuhan* presents the various character possibilities of modernization without seriously showing the dynamics of modernization. For this we must turn to another film.

DESA DI KAKI BUKIT

Desa Di Kaki Bukit (The Village at the Foot of the Hills), like *Salah Asuhan,* was directed by Asrul Sani, but it was not based on a famous book and apparently is not even well remembered today. Set in the early 1980s, it is the story of the opening of a small Javanese village, Semangka ("Watermelon"), to the outside world. The film begins with the ceremonial ribbon-cutting of the new bridge. Soon a bus enters the village, bringing a school-teacher, a midwife, a prostitute, and a jack-of-all-trades scoun-drel. Modernization begins, but it is opposed by the village head who realizes that with birth control his wife will produce fewer children to work his tobacco fields, and if the children spend their days in school they will not be hoeing tobacco. Finally, when his son excels in school and the midwife saves his wife's life, the head-man is converted to modernization and all make progress together happily ever after.

Said, the village headman, begins the film as Traditional-Indo-nesian and ends it as fairly Modern-Indonesian. (See Figure 2.) At first he is a stubborn advocate for conservatism: What was good then is good now. The accursed bridge brings only snakes and insects. If city people are so smart, let them solve their own prob-lems. Even when the schoolteacher points out that the bridge could also be used to take Said's tobacco to market, he is unmoved. He shows no concern for his wife's difficult labor; when called to her bedside, he jokes that there is nothing he can do in the birthing. He rides around the countryside on a small horse supervising his laborers—who include his frail wife and his many

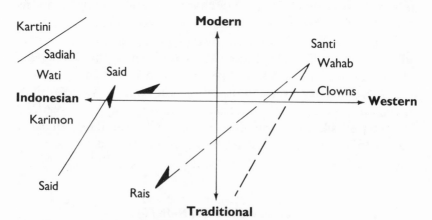

Figure 2. The Modernization Grid: *Desa Di Kaki Bukit*
(The Village at the Foot of the Hills)

children. He sees both the school and the clinic as plots to deprive him of his work force. Soon he orders both school and clinic to be boarded up and has the schoolteacher beaten.

Characters seldom undergo gradual transformations in Indonesian films; rather, they experience sudden conversions. Said is no exception. Because of his actions, the school has been forced to meet outdoors. But when Said overhears his oldest son, Hasan, answering the teacher's questions correctly he swells with pride and proclaims a brilliant future for his son as a government official. Immediately afterward, his weakened wife collapses in the tobacco fields and he is forced to call in the midwife, who saves her life. From then on, Said is an advocate of modernity: He has leapt from the Traditional-Indonesian to the Modern-Indonesian. We see him leading his horse with his wife on its back while he himself walks; we see him as an ally of the midwife, shocked to see her leaving the village, relieved that she is coming back immediately. And in a final joke, he waxes indignant when hearing about a conservative headman nearby and then finally realizes that the story is about him—or, rather, about his former self.

Rais, the new schoolteacher, has made two major movements in terms of character type before the film opens. We learn that he grew up in a village, presumably in a Traditional-Indonesian setting. But then, when he lived in Jakarta, he became very Modern-Western and had a torrid affair with Santi. Now, however, he has come to the village at the foot of the hills to serve the people as schoolteacher. He talks about his mission with great patriotic and moral fervor. He is clearly now Modern-Indonesian—actually a rare male character in this type. His movement is best illustrated when he definitively rejects Santi and marries a village girl, Wati.

Wati is close to being a young version of the Kartini figure. She is very much a Modern-Indonesian type: She is well educated and a schoolteacher. (One of the slight awkwardnesses of the plot is that there already was a village school, with two teachers, even before the bus brought Rais in over the new bridge.) She is the daughter of the ferryboatman. And her appearance is right—she is a classic Indonesian beauty and dresses only in traditional Indonesian clothing. But she is modern: In a nice touch, when her mother remarks on her fingernail polish, Wati replies that "Girls do that these days, Mom." (She uses the traditional word *gadis*—girl, maiden, even virgin.) Only her central role as young protagonist instead of middle-aged peripheral catalyzer keeps Wati from being a true Kartini figure.

It is Sadiah, the midwife who came into the village on the bus with the others, who plays the real Kartini role. Traditionally beautiful, traditionally dressed, a decade older than Wati, Sadiah is a widow with children in school far away, but now she is dedicated to helping the village. She uses her expertise as a midwife nurse, and she acts as advisor and confidante to Rais, the schoolteacher. She is the full Kartini type and plays that figure's order-restoring role.

Santi, Rais's former lover, arrives in her sports car from Jakarta dressed in tight blouse and slacks. She intends to take Rais back to their Jakarta love nest. When she realizes that he has changed and she has a rival in Wati, she turns on Wati and tries to embarrass her in front of Rais: "Why don't you introduce me to this village girl, Rais? Or maybe you are ashamed because her hands reek of mud!" But Rais has nailed Santi in her Modern-Western corner as he recalls their life together: "You with your false eyelashes and your fake hair, me with the wealth my father gave me, we floated on a dream that wasn't even ours." After an unconvincing moment of understanding how Rais has changed and what he is up to in the village, Santi leaves. But she represents the rejected type —the false modernization.

There is a third schoolteacher, a young man named Wahab, who plays an exemplary negative role as a Modern-Western character type. He is the true bureaucrat who draws his salary no matter what. He will teach if there are children, but he is perfectly content if there are no children. Wati asks him, "Just what are your responsibilities as a teacher?" and he answers, "What are you asking for? I just want to get along with my boss." Whereas Santi's Modern-Western failings lie in the area of self-indulgent sexuality, Wahab's lie in social irresponsibility. Between the two of them, they nicely box the possibilities of this type.

Karimun, the old ferryboatman who is Wati's father, in a sense parallels Said's transformation, but without the drama of conversion. The first shots of the film cut back and forth between Karimun on the river, taking his last load of peasants across in his boat, and the officials and villagers ceremoniously cutting the ribbon and opening the new bridge. The bridge destroys Karimun's ferryboat business, of course, but he is quietly accepting and approving of the progress. (And, as some villagers point out, he does have the salary of his daughter the schoolteacher.) Never as extreme nor as vehement as Said, Karimun gently moves toward the Modern end of the Indonesian zone.

In some ways the most interesting characters are Usman (the scoundrelly jack-of-all-trades) and the prostitute. They arrive on the same bus as the schoolteacher and the midwife and immediately settle in. They work various scams, usually unsuccessfully. (When Usman tries to sell fertility medicine to the headman just after his wife miscarries, he is thrown into a water tank for his poor timing.) In the end, though, they set up a legitimate photography business and announce their intention to get married. In an interesting and very Indonesian way these two figures parallel the schoolteacher's earlier transformation from Modern-Western to Modern-Indonesian types. But while Rais remains upper class and refined—even his description of his affair with Santi in Jakarta is poetic—these two characters are coarse throughout. The well-known Indonesian dichotomy between refined *(alus)* and coarse *(kasar)* is nicely exemplified here.

But even more, Usman and the prostitute are very Indonesian clowns. In the Western theatrical traditions—Shakespeare, for example—there are clowns who echo, ridicule, and comment upon the actions of their betters. Likewise in classical Indonesian theater. And here, in this movie, we see the clown roles played by Usman and the prostitute. They are the *kasar* versions of Rais and Wati. Although there was no prior relationship between Rais and Usman before they met on the bus (in Shakespeare Usman would have been cast as Rais's servant), they are often in the same scenes and confer together on a quite serious level. Usman, in particular, sounds like the *ludruk* clowns which Peacock describes: "The clown owns no property and so is sometimes shown wandering homeless, but unlike Western literary tramps . . . the clown never wanders by himself: he is always with a partner, yet he never appears to empathize or identify with his partner and will betray him in an instant. . . . He . . . mocks his master's external signs —sounds and motions. The clown's favorite game is to imitate gestures and words of somebody other than himself . . ." (Peacock 1987:73).

As a model for modernization which leads an audience to

explore the possibilities of personality type and action in a modernizing world, *Desa Di Kaki Bukit* (The Village at the Foot of the Hills) is far richer than *Salah Asuhan* (Wrong Upbringing). The conceptual framework of the two axes—Traditional/Modern and Indonesian/Western—affords us access to a level beyond the gross plot line. Although I do not claim that any Indonesian filmmaker had this particular conceptual scheme in mind when making his film, I do think the scheme would be immediately recognizable as an accurate description of the characters. In fact, after I had completed this analysis of *Desa Di Kaki Bukit,* the director, Asrul Sani, told me that the film had been sponsored by the national family planning board and hence was intended as a model of modernization.

LIMITS TO THE GRID

Development of plot, or development of character, is shown as movement across the grid. Movement, if it exists at all in these films, is almost always toward the Modern-Indonesian quadrant. One of the very rare exceptions occurs in *Carok* (Duel), which is a sort of *Godfather* film set, significantly, in Madura (which, in important ways, is the Sicily of Indonesia). The young son of the Family is sent to the university, where he begins to write a dissertation on the sociology of violence. When his older brother is killed he is drawn back to the Family business as *capo/kepala,* turning from analyzer to organizer of violence. But it is difficult to find other examples of such retrograde movement.

These two axes differ considerably from each other. The Modern/Traditional axis has ideological and technological implications: education, literacy, health care, family planning. The Indonesian/Western axis, on the other hand, has a moral implication: The Western end is the locus of moral corruption, sexuality, drinking, social irresponsibility; the Indonesian end is the locus of honesty, modesty, sobriety, social responsibility. Together the two axes form the grid on which people in movies play out their lives and try to solve that most difficult of all Indonesian problems: how to modernize and yet retain Indonesian identity; how to avoid the perils of excessive conservatism on the one hand and destructive Western-ness on the other.

There remain two loose ends which should be discussed here even if briefly. The approach presented throughout this book is a genre approach. That is, we are less concerned with the individual films of particular directors than with treating films in terms of their common formulaic qualities. Thus I have treated "Indonesian" films as almost a folk genre. This approach works with many Indonesian films, as with many Western films. But it does leave unanalyzed certain unusual films which, although they deal with modernization, do so by violating the formula.

Take, for example, the mid-1970s film *Cintaku Di Kampus Biru* (My Love on the Blue Campus), made from a well-known novel by Ashadi Siregar. This is a political allegory using campus politics to deal with challenges to authority and with Inner Island/Outer Island conflict. The same grid that was useful for analyzing the various genre films is inadequate here. Not only would nearly everyone be clustered in the same area (very Modern, moderately Western), but the conflicts and movements do not take place in terms of this grid at all. In fact, there is a character who clearly fits the Kartini figure described above, but she turns out to be the epitome of Javanese feudalism against which the Menado student unsuccessfully pits himself. The point is that just as the techniques of understanding folktales do not work well with novels, so the techniques of understanding genre films often fail with auteur films.

A second loose end: The case has been made here for treating these films as guidebooks, in a sense, for personal types and actions in that process of change we call modernization—and particularly for the ways in which the films celebrate the Indonesianization of modernization. Indonesian films do not exist in a vacuum. In the movie theaters and videocassette rental shops throughout the country, films produced in Indonesia make up perhaps a third of the offerings. There are many competing films from China, India, Europe, and especially the United States. For each film of the type I have analyzed in this chapter, most young Indonesians will probably see several films from America which celebrate a thoroughly Western, thoroughly American, sort of modernization where the leading characters indulge in sex, liquor, and individualistic social irresponsibility. (The *Rambo* and *Rocky* series were exceptionally popular in Indonesia during the 1980s.)

How can one understand the effect of this complex mix of

media input on individual Indonesians? On the one hand, there
are the Indonesian films which promote a certain view of modernization. But how are they balanced by the foreign films which
present the opposite view? And then, to further complicate the
equation, I suspect that the plot and character subtleties of the
Western films are really not understood by most Indonesian audiences. Ward Keeler has noted a similar situation with Western television programs (1987:139), and A. L. Becker remarks that different members of a *wayang* audience will attend or doze off at
different parts of the performance (1979:230).

Throughout this book I have been treating Indonesian films as
texts to be analyzed from a cultural standpoint. Especially in this
chapter the emphasis is on what the texts communicate. Although
I advance assumptions about what audiences actually make of it
all, I do not pretend to have actual data on audiences. The next
step would be to treat as a whole the visual world of modern Indonesia, including film and television, domestic and imports. What
do Indonesians construct out of it? Then we would be approach-
ing "popular culture" in the sense that John Fiske means when he
writes of the "repertoire of texts or cultural resources for the various formations of the people to use or reject in the ongoing process of producing their popular culture" (1989a:24). And we need
to take seriously Fiske's argument that "popular texts are inadequate in themselves—they are never self-sufficient structures of
meanings . . . they are provokers of meanings and pleasure, they
are completed only when taken up by people and inserted into
their everyday culture" (1989b:6).

PHOTO 1   Movie advertisements from *Majalah Film* (Film Magazine) showing some of the different film genres: *Brahmana Manggala,* a historic epic . . .

PHOTO 2   *Sang Primadona,* a youth film . . .

PHOTO 3   *Keluarga Markum*, a comedy.

PHOTO 4   A downtown Jakarta movie theater advertising two American films and *Sundelbolong,* an Indonesian horror film.

PHOTO 5   A standard motif: A dying patient being pulled in a gurney along a hospital breezeway in *Perempuan Dalam Pasungan* (The Woman in Stocks). (Courtesy Sinematek Indonesia Archive)

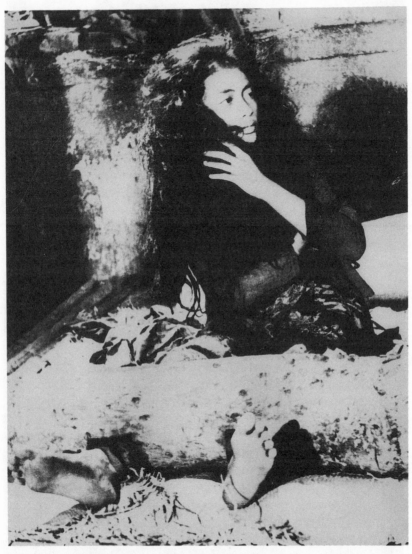

PHOTO 6 Nungki Kusumastuti, who has gone mad, is locked in stocks in *Perempuan Dalam Pasungan.* This is a powerful image of someone who has fallen into extreme disorder and must be straightened out. Her loose hair emphasizes her mental disorder. (Courtesy Sinematek Indonesia Archive)

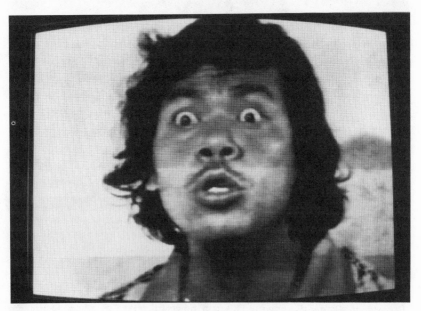

Photos 7 and 8   The two anger faces that appear in Indonesian life and films: Brows down *(top),* the pan-cultural version, and brows up *(bottom),* the Indonesian emblem for anger. Both expressions made by Benyamin S. during the course of a single scene in *Raja Copet* (King of the Pickpockets).

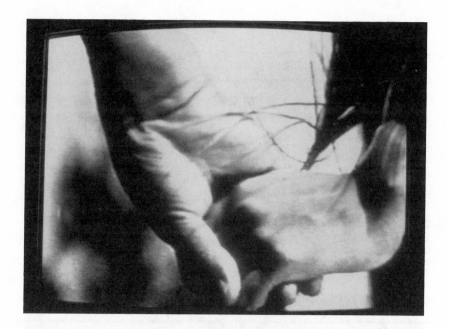

PHOTOS 9 and 10   Two resolutions to the problem of how to hold hands without making palm-to-palm contact between a right and a left hand: In *Desa 'Di Kaki Bukit* (The Village at the Foot of the Hills, *top*), the two schoolteachers have just declared their love and the camera comes in on their hands. In *Salah Asuhan* (Wrong Upbringing, *bottom*), husband and wife are reunited and reconciled at her deathbed.

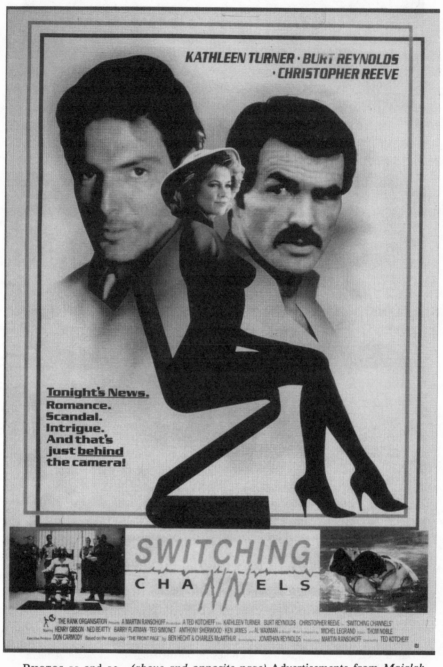

PHOTOS 11 and 12 *(above and opposite page)* Advertisements from *Majalah Film* for imported American movies, with their emphasis on female sexuality.

Peter Coyote
Greta Scacchi

A MAN IN LOVE

PETER COYOTE   GRETA SCACCHI   VINCENT LINDON

Director of Photography BERNARD ZITZERMANN   Art Director DEAN TAVOULARIS   Music GEORGES DELERUE
Original screenplay DIANE KURYS   Associate Producers MARJORIE ISRAEL   ARMAND BARBAULT
G   Director MICHEL SEYDOUX   DIANE KURYS   Director DIANE KURYS   DOLBY STEREO

PHOTO 13   Indonesian films, by contrast, often use advertising that focuses on the family life of stars, as in this poster sold in the markets.

PHOTO 14   Rima Melati as the beautiful but unsophisticated Minangkabau girl and Fifi Young as her mother-in-law in *Salah Asuhan*. (Courtesy Sinematek Indonesia Archive)

CHAPTER 7

MOVING PICTURES, MOVING HISTORIES

One way of thinking about historical films is to ask how accurate they are. The answer is invariably "not very." Filmmakers are not historians. There may be close collaborations, as when Natalie Zemon Davis guided the making of the 1982 French film *The Return of Martin Guerre,* but these are rare. Fiction films certainly communicate something of history and may even be helpful in teaching, but they do not meet the standards of historical accuracy.

Somehow, whenever a feature film has a historical setting, people approach it as if it were a Ph.D. dissertation and get carried away with questions of its historical accuracy. The reviewer for the *Jakarta Post,* Jeremy Allan (12 October 1985), called *Doea Tanda Mata* (Mementos) "good cinema, bad history." It is certainly legitimate to ask about the accuracy of a film. But if we acknowledge that any history must be more or less a latter-day construct, we can go beyond errors of detail and look at the sort of past which is being provided for the present. In this case, two major historical errors have been pointed out by Allan, quoting Dr. Onghokham, lecturer in Indonesian social history at the University of Indonesia: The killings of nationalists by Dutch troops happened rarely if ever in Java; and the clandestine nature of the nationalistic pamphlet-publishing venture is exaggerated, for in the 1930s such publications were public (if often short-lived). The effect of these "errors" is to make the 1930s movement seem more dangerous and thus more heroic—and so to extend the history of the Perjuangan, a term meaning "struggle," which is usually meant to refer to the armed resistance of the 1945–1949 period. Many Indonesian films about the Japanese occupation of the early 1940s show groups of Indonesian freedom fighters attacking the Japanese forces. Now, in *Doea Tanda Mata,* the Perjuangan is given even earlier roots in the 1930s.

BEYOND HISTORICAL ACCURACY

Teguh Karya, the film's director, does not talk about "historical accuracy." In an unpublished interview with John McGlynn about *Doea Tanda Mata,* Teguh characterizes the film with two words— *tamsil* and *perumpamaan,* which mean parable or example—and has called it *semacam metafor* ("a sort of metaphor"). Thus we can pose a much more interesting question. The basic premise of this book is that films reflect their culture. We can now refine this premise to say that historical films reflect present understandings of time past. This is particularly evident if we compare the ways in which two films of different periods treat the same event of the past.

A familiar American example is the film treatments of the battle on the Little Bighorn River on 25 June 1976. The early treatments presented General Custer as hero—a tragic victim of fate. By the late 1960s, however, two major political movements were occupying the minds of Americans: The United States began to reject the earlier patterns of discrimination against minority groups, including Native Americans, and the disastrous war in Vietnam brought the military into disrepute among many sectors of the American population. These two movements, or changing conceptions, were reflected in the films of the period which dealt with the Indian Wars—films like *Soldier Blue* (1970) about the Sand Creek Massacre and *Little Big Man* (also 1970) where Custer was portrayed as a madman intent on killing Indians for his personal glory. Hollywood was not courageously presenting the case for Indians or the case against war. It was making films which reflected new readings of the Indian Wars and the military—perceptions held by large numbers of the ticket-buying American public. There are of course many better and more detailed sources for information on this change of historical understanding. And the movies give rather unnuanced sketches of history. But movies are powerful and more responsive to public culture than are the monographs of historians. So they provide valuable clues about contemporary views of the past. And this is especially true in Indonesia, where films must be sensitive both to public taste and to the government censorship board.

A good Indonesian example of changing conceptions is the way in which two films from different eras treat the Perjuangan, the struggle for independence. One of the most celebrated incidents in the Struggle was the briefly successful Republican army attack on Yogyakarta. This court city in Central Java had been the capital of the Republican government. Then, on 19 December 1948, the Dutch forces broke the so-called Renville Truce, attacked Yogyakarta, and captured the Republican leaders, Sukarno and Hatta. But the sultan, Hamengku Buwono IX, was a strong supporter of the revolution and maintained contact with the Republican forces surrounding Yogyakarta. Although the Republican army could not hope to defeat the Dutch army in direct battle, it could embarrass the Dutch with small noisy skirmishes. And by the end of 1949 this strategy had tipped international opinion against the Dutch and the Indonesians had won complete independence.

By breaking the truce in December 1948, the Dutch had played a risky game. They knew that world opinion would be against them, but at least they thought they could crush the heart of the revolution. They miscalculated. The Republican government was able to carry on, the sultan remained loyal to the revolution, and, most dramatically, in January the Republican army made a daring raid into the heart of Yogyakarta and held it for a few hours. They were soon driven out again, but it was a Pyrrhic victory for the Dutch (not unlike the 1971 Tet Offensive of the Vietnamese War). The date of the attack was "the night of 9 January" according to George Kahin, who was there (1952:395) and 1 March according to O. G. Roeder, who was not (1969:121).

One of the participants in this attack was Suharto, then a lieutenant colonel and now president of the republic. The attack was mentioned briefly in George Kahin's 1952 history. In 1951, barely two years after the event, Usmar Ismail made a film about it called *Enam Djam Di Jogya* (Six Hours in Jogja). Neither film nor book specifically mentions Suharto, and in the film it is the sultan who is the most prominent hero of the attack. But in later years, after Suharto became president, there was more interest in his role as a young officer in the revolution. In 1983 Arifin C. Noer made *Sarangan Fajar* (Attack at Dawn) in which he retold the story of the Yogyakarta attack, but this time with Suharto sharing center stage with the sultan. And although *Sarangan Fajar* won several Citra awards in 1983, the earlier film, *Enam Djam Di Jogja,* was still being shown on the single government television channel in the 1980s.

Rewriting history on the basis of retrospective interest in the early days of a national hero is certainly not limited to Indonesian films: American cinema has *Young Mr. Lincoln* (1939) and, more directly analogous, *PT 109* (1963) about Lt. (j.g.) John F. Kennedy's exploits during World War II. *Sarangan Fajar* is mild hagiography to be sure, and certainly no one has suggested that Suharto did not take part in the 1949 Yogyakarta raid. But his role has perhaps been retrospectively redefined.

THE LONG MARCH

A more complex example of filming and refilming history centers on the "Long March" of the Siliwangi Division. After the Renville agreement of January 1948 had partitioned Java between Republican and Dutch forces, the Siliwangi Division withdrew from its home base in West Java to the Republican zone in Central Java. But when the Dutch broke the truce in December 1948 with their attack on Yogyakarta, the division was ordered back to West Java. As George Kahin describes it, "their way was bitterly contested not only by the Dutch but by the troops of Darul Islam as well" (1952:409). Darul Islam was a well-organized movement based in West Java which attempted to establish an Indonesian Islamic state (Jackson and Moeliono 1973; Jackson 1980). Thus it was hostile to the Republican government, which was committed to an inclusive secular Indonesian nation. And when the Republicans signed the Renville agreement with the Dutch and withdrew their forces from West Java, Darul Islam repudiated Renville and dug in. Not surprisingly, when the breakdown of the truce sent the Siliwangi Division back to West Java, a three-way struggle broke out between the Dutch, the Republicans, and Darul Islam. In the end the Dutch were sent home and the movement for an Islamic state was effectively, although not totally, suppressed. The Republicans prevailed to rule the archipelago and thus, of course, to license the writing and filming of the history of these events.

Two films were made of the Long March. The first, *Darah Dan*

Do'a (Blood and Prayer), by Usmar Ismail, was released in 1950, barely eighteen months after the event itself. *Darah Dan Do'a* was given the subtitle (in English!) of "The Long March," evoking the Long March of the Chinese People's Army of 1934–1935. *Darah Dan Do'a* was one of twenty-four Indonesian films released in 1950, the first year of independence and peace, but it is the only one which survives. In fact, it is the oldest known Indonesian film still extant. The other film, *Mereka Kembali* (They Return), was made by Imam Tontowi in 1975, twenty-five years after the event, in an Indonesia with quite different concerns.

We can compare these two films in terms of how they handle both the core military event and then (in Chapter 10) the concomitant personal complications. In one sense these films tell the history of the Siliwangi Division. But while *Mereka Kembali* begins with the Dutch attack of 19 December, *Darah Dan Do'a* starts with the Madiun Affair. In September 1948, during the Renville Truce, the Communist Party of Indonesia and sympathetic Republican troops based in the Central Javanese city of Madiun attempted a military coup to gain control of the Republican government. The uprising was put down by other Republican troops loyal to the Hatta government, most notably the Siliwangi Division (see Kahin 1952:290 ff.). But the social cost was high. David Charles Anderson writes: "The atrocities . . . were so appalling in their magnitude and intensity that they could only have been committed by groups roused to highly volatile states of religious and political fervor" (1976:45, 46).

Darah Dan Do'a, made in the immediate wake of Madiun, incorporates it as the karmic force of the plot. The film opens with a Siliwangi unit capturing and then slaughtering a Communist unit at Madiun. The Siliwangi officer, Sudarto, although he did not exactly order the shooting of the prisoners, was responsible for it, and at the end of the movie he is killed in revenge by a relative of one of the Communist officers. While the champions of the films are unquestionably the Republican Siliwangi men, it is significant that in 1952 the Communists are not pictured as monsters. Since they have been treated unjustly, the act of final revenge is quite understandable.

The later film, *Mereka Kembali,* ignores Madiun completely and begins with the Dutch attack and the Long March. But once the march gets under way, both films include similar scenes:

The Long March begins from Central Java with the iconic
tenth-century Hindu-Buddhist monuments as backdrops. (In
Darah Dan Do'a the Siliwangi Division marches west, past
Borobudur, but in *Mereka Kembali* it is shown, unaccount-
ably, marching past Prambanum eastward!)
The Siliwangi troops are accompanied by their families. This is
not an epic of male bonding—the entire society participates.
It is a village on the move. Kahin describes the Long March in
these terms: "Marching in units of one or two battalions and
often with the wives and children of the men in the rear the
Siliwangi Division fought its way some 200 miles through cen-
tral and part of West Java" (1952:409).
The capture of the Republican leaders, Sukarno and Hatta,
shakes the troops but they march on.
The troops sing college-outing-type songs.
They are attacked by Dutch airplanes.
A woman gives birth.

But the opposition to the Siliwangi Division's progress is significantly different in the two films: In *Darah Dan Do'a* the division
has to fight only against the Dutch and an occasional village collaborator; in *Mereka Kembali* the real struggle is with the Darul
Islam forces. According to Kahin (1952:330) the Darul Islam army
included not only Muslim leaders but also opportunistic guerrillas
and even "many of the old-time professional bandit gangs of the
area." In the film, Darul Islam is represented by the bandit element only—shaggy dirty wild warriors who attack the Siliwangi
Division by poisoning the food at a village feast and killing peace
envoys. The only thing at all Islamic about them is the green and
white flag sometimes shown in the background. Significantly there
are several manifestations of religion, both Islam and Christianity,
in the Siliwangi ranks, but none in the Darul Islam ranks.

A QUESTION OF TREATMENT

Historically both the Madiun Affair and the conflict with Darul
Islam are part of the Siliwangi story. Both are dramatic incidents
fit for an action film. Is such incorporation or exclusion, then,
merely a matter of aesthetic choice? Or can we draw historical significance from it?

It is inevitably perilous to push this sort of cultural analysis beyond the simple noting of differences. As an insider I feel confident about the interpretation of different American film treatments of the nineteenth-century Indian Wars. As an outsider I am considerably less confident about identifying nuances of Indonesian political culture. (Salim Said, an Indonesian film scholar, has discussed these same films with a different emphasis [1990].) Short of explicit statements of intention by directors and scriptwriters—which I do not have and doubt that I could get—we must build a case from circumstantial evidence. But let us try.

The first problem is this: Why the sensitive treatment of Communists at Madiun in *Darah Dan Do'a* but the total omission of Madiun in *Mereka Kembali?* Perhaps 1951 was a time for healing, a time to consolidate the new republic, to reincorporate even those who, like the Communists, had fought against it. Madiun was indeed a "haunting experience" (D. C. Anderson 1976:45). This film treatment was a way of bringing it gently and comprehensively to closure. But by 1975 the event of 30 September 1965, called the GESTAPU Affair, which evoked the Madiun Affair in so many ways, overshadowed every other consideration. Madiun could not be treated sympathetically without appearing to condone and excuse GESTAPU. But GESTAPU was still too sensitive to be dealt with in any way—it would be several years before the first films on the subject would begin to appear. So by the mid-1970s Madiun, because of its resonances, could not be uttered.

The second problem is the reverse: Why was Darul Islam treated so negatively in 1975 but ignored in 1951? Perhaps by 1975 the government no longer felt any real threat from the Communists, since the party had been so thoroughly rooted out in the aftermath of the GESTAPU Affair. The major internal threat was the pressure to turn the secular Republic of Indonesia, in which all religions had nominal equality, into an Islamic republic. Although Darul Islam itself had ended in 1961, many of the more conservative Muslim factions were still maneuvering for a stronger Islamic direction to the republic and resented what they perceived as the secularization of Suharto's New Order.

In this political context, *Mereka Kembali* makes two strong statements: First, it attacks Darul Islam by showing them as crazed treacherous bandits devoid of religious feelings: second, it shows the Republican Siliwangi Division as being actually quite religious. The troops—both men and women—are a true cross-section of Indonesia and, before going into battle, the officer requests each to pray in his or her own way. The camera pans along the row of soldiers praying in Christian as well as Muslim attitudes. (Earlier a Chinese soldier had died a noble death.) But at the end of the film, as the hero is buried in a Muslim ceremony, the camera tilts upward for the final nationalist word to show the red and white flag of the republic standing beside the sacred banner of the Siliwangi Division which had been preserved from the Darul Islam bandits.

In summary, each film is a history lesson for its time. This is not to accuse the films of actually falsifying history. Rather, out of the myriad facts which surround Siliwangi and the Long March, each film has selected a few to emphasize. The two pictures are different, but each is explained by the demands of its political moment.

We can also compare the ways in which the two films handle their peripheral romantic subplots. In *Darah Dan Do'a,* the hero Sudarto is attracted to a German woman. He helps her, eventually is captured while visiting her, and then she inconclusively vanishes from the story. But in *Mereka Kembali* the two girls are at first encouraged by their comfortable middle-class father to flirt with Dutch officers. Their mother, a strong modern Indonesian Kartini figure, finally puts her foot down and shames the father into supporting the revolution. The girls buy medicine and carry it over the hills and rivers to the Siliwangi Division. There the younger daughter is reunited with her fiancé, an officer, and the older girl falls in love with the sergeant, who is the real hero of the story. But love does not hold either man back from combat. The sergeant dies heroically (in a Wild West village street shootout with the one-eyed Darul Islam bandit leader) and the officer, no less heroic, is wounded, perhaps fatally.

The subplot of *Darah Dan Do'a* is rather inconclusive, but it does present a European in a favorable light. Later films about the Struggle have smoothed things out and there are no sympathetic Europeans. The subplot of *Mereka Kembali* is more interesting. It resolves a problem which is mentioned, if not resolved, in most films about the revolution—the fact that many Indonesians supported the Dutch to the end. Their careers, their very lives, were inextricably bound to the Dutch and it was hard to break those bonds. Soldiers, government officials, the middle class—all had many reasons not to gamble on the Republicans. (It is said of

South Carolinians during the American Revolution that a third were pro-revolution, a third were royalists, and a third sat on the fence.)

In *Mereka Kembali* the father is plump and comfortable, smokes a pipe, and accepts gifts from the Dutch officers who are courting his daughters. His wife is the true patriot. When she puts a stop to his collaboration and offers her gold ornaments for the revolution, her daughters agree with quick relief. The husband then comes around, albeit grudgingly. But the girls joyfully fall on him and proclaim him a hero. Eventually the Dutch find out about the girls running medicine to the Siliwangi men. But when they arrive to confiscate the house, they find that he has sold it overnight to innocent Chinese in order to foil them. Thus the subplot resolves the collaborator problem: He is turned into a revolutionary by the force of his wife's strong character.

While it is obviously fruitless to approach these historical films as sources of historical data, they do show us how the society—perhaps we should say the government—actively works on the past and uses it to give certain kinds of meanings to the present. And it is safe to predict that these events of the 1940s, so pivotal in the Indonesian experience, will be further reworked in the Indonesian films of the future.

CHAPTER 8

CONSTRUCTING THE OTHER: FOLK ETHNOGRAPHY

Most films do not stretch their audience's imagination very far. Familiar sorts of people confront familiar sorts of problems in familiar sorts of settings. Of course, everything is cranked up a notch or two: The people are more beautiful, the problems more intense, and the settings more elegant than normal. And then there are films which deal with quite exotic people. The most obvious genres are Historical films which deal with people of the past, Horror films which deal with transformed and supernatural (and subnatural?) creatures, and Legend films which deal with more or less mythic beings. Curiously, the Science Fiction genre—which deals with the ultimate exotics, namely, beings from outer space—does not seem to be made by Indonesians at all. Considering how important this genre has been in the West—Georges Melies, the great French pioneer, made one of his first movies about *A Trip to the Moon* in 1902—it is surprising that Indonesians neglect it. There are no obvious cultural reasons for this neglect.

In this chapter we look at how Indonesian cinema depicts tribal peoples. We ask how Indonesian cinema constructs The Other. From the perspective of metropolitan Indonesians, each ethnic group is to some extent strange and The Other. But for all Indonesians of the core—and that means the moviegoing public—the really different peoples are those tribal folk who live in isolated parts of Sumatra, Kalimantan (Borneo), and especially Irian Jaya (New Guinea). These dark-skinned, "primitif" pagans pose special problems of representation.

CONSTRUCTING THE OTHER: SOME POSSIBILITIES

Anthropologists have mixed feelings about the extent to which they "construct" others. Ethnographic descriptions should be reasonably neutral and realistic, neither exaggerating nor denying differences. The goal is to present other cultures in their own terms but to make them understandable to everyone. In fact, this is a kind of naive positivism. Even anthropologists construct others for a variety of reasons (see Heider 1990) and often bias their accounts toward the exotic details (see Keesing 1989). But anthropologists do have an obligation to at least try for some sort of accuracy in their pictures of The Other. Feature films, on the other hand, are not so constrained. Films must make money by telling entertaining stories. While films do have many constraints, they are not impeded in the same way by these anthropological considerations. And as they must have at least a moderate popular appeal, they draw from the popular culture their ideas about the world.

There are three obvious strategies that film directors may choose in constructing The Other. The first is to deny the differences—which is to say, deny the Otherness. This is the "Family of Man" approach, named after that sentimental collection of photographs supposed to show that all humans are basically alike. To the extent that it affirmed the essential humanity of all peoples, it was admirable. To the extent that it denied the essential and very real differences between cultures, it was misleading.

An example of this stategy is the 1936 American film *Mary Queen of Scots*. Set in the sixteenth century, the film is about Mary Stewart, pretender to the English throne occupied by Elizabeth. Mary was exotic even for sixteenth-century England—a Catholic, raised in France, probably speaking some broken form of English which was neither the Queen's nor the Scots'. For an American mid-1930s audience she was potentially even more exotic. But in the movie she is acted by Katherine Hepburn as a simpering Philadelphia coed with a strong American accent. Her Otherness denied, she was made one of us.

But this is the least exciting strategy. On the whole, filmmakers (and anthropologists!) reject this approach and opt to construct some sort of *real* Other. Western cinema has two cultural proto-

types of the Other to draw on: the Noble Savage and the Ignoble
Savage.

The Noble Savage

From antiquity, European cultures have had an idea of peoples or
cultures far away or long ago who lived a simpler, better life, close
to nature, unspoiled by the complications of civilization. This general idea has been called "primitivism." Lovejoy and Boas (1965)
distinguish "chronological primitivism," which speaks of a past
Golden Age, from "cultural primitivism," which speaks of Noble
Savages. While the classical world spoke of the Golden Age, the
Noble Savage was a more modern conception stimulated by the
great age of European exploration and imperial expansion. In
Hoxie Neale Fairchild's formulation, "a Noble Savage is any free
and wild being who draws directly from nature virtues which raise
doubts as to the value of civilization" (1928:2).

A memorable early cinematic appearance of Noble Savages was
in Robert Flaherty's documentary film of Samoa, *Moana* (1928).
Significantly, Flaherty's own subtitle for the film was "A Romance of the Golden Age." Flaherty idealized the Samoans, their
culture, and their environment. He showed them immune from all
the problems of the northern civilization which had sent Flaherty
to Samoa and then thronged to see the movie when it played in
their northern cities.

The Ignoble Savage

But if the Noble Savage is the idealistic version of the extreme
Other, there is another possibility: the extreme negative version in
which the lack of civilization reveals not the natural good in
humans but the natural bad. These people are far from noble.
They are wild men—barbarians. There is a stock figure of the
Wild Man represented in the art and literature of the European
Middle Ages who is traditionally covered with hair, carries a large
club, and often wears a leafy loin covering. According to Richard
Bernheimer, wildness "implied everything that eluded Christian
norms and the established framework of Christian society, referring to what was uncanny, unruly, raw, unpredictable, foreign,
uncultured and uncultivated" (1952:20). Hayden White observed

that the Roman and Medieval worlds "conceived barbarians and wild men to be enslaved to nature, to be, like animals, slaves to desire and unable to control these passions; as mobile, shifting, confused, chaotic; as incapable of sedentary existence, of self-discipline, and of sustained labor; as passionate, bewildered, and hostile to 'normal' humanity" (1972:20).

These, then, are the two prototypical forms into which the West has cast its tribal outliers. We are talking about popular conceptions and popular literature. As might be expected, the elite literature has avoided the trap of the prototype and has dealt with these Others in more nuanced terms. Leo Marx (1964) has observed that in both Shakespeare's *Tempest* and Melville's *Typee,* what begins with Noble Savages living in tropical paradises turns to horror with the discovery that the people are actually dangerous cannibals.

But here we are looking at prototypes—cultural stereotypes. Just as the West turns some tribal peoples into Noble Savages of the *Moana* sort, they also turn others into barbarians, quite Ignoble Savages. If *Moana* typifies the Noble Savage, another famous film of the period, *King Kong* (1933), gives us barbarians. *King Kong* was out-and-out fiction, of course. A documentary film expedition sails to The Island, which lies to the southwest of Sumatra, looking for the great ape Kong. The natives of the island are dark-skinned savages who propitiate Kong by presenting him with village girls (undoubtedly virgins) in regular ceremonies. Knowing a good thing when they see it, they snatch the beautiful American girl from the expedition ship and give her to Kong, who is suitably appreciative. These savages in the background are not of much significance except to move the plot along. We learn little of them in their brief scenes except that they are dark-skinned, wear furs, feathers, and paint, seem to be led by a witch doctor, and give their daughters up as blackmail payments to Kong.

INDONESIAN CONSTRUCTS

Indonesian films depict no Golden Age. There are films set in the ancient but historical kingdoms like Madjapahit or Srivijaya, but they hardly depict a simple noble folk close to nature. Rather, they tell stories of warring kingdoms, palace intrigue, great heroes, and their supernatural helpers. When Indonesian films do depict tribal peoples, they are shown very much as barbarians: Ignoble Savages.

Several Indonesian films deal with tribal peoples. *Intan Perawan Kubu* (The Virgin of Kubu) is about an expedition to Jambi, in Sumatra, which is set upon by howling savages. In *Dia Sang Penakluk* (She the Conqueror) a spoiled rich girl gets involved with a medical mission to the Dani in Irian Jaya. But the most telling example is in the comparison of two versions of the same film: the 1975 American version of *Blue Lagoon* and the 1980 Indonesian remake of the same film, called *Pengantin Pantai Biru* (The Bride of the Blue Shore). *Blue Lagoon* actually was taken from a novel by Henry DeVere Stacpoole published in England in 1908. It was first filmed in England in 1949, starring Jean Simmons. We shall discuss it again in Chapter 10, but for the moment let us just compare the savages in the two most recent movie versions. The plot is simple: Two children cast ashore on a tropical island survive, grow up, learn about love, have a baby, and are rescued. In both films there is an encounter with a tribe, and in both cases the tribe is barbaric.

In the American version, the children hear distant drumbeats but are warned not to investigate by the ship's cook, who has lived long enough to teach them basic survival skills. Years later the boy does follow the sound of the drums. He creeps through the jungle and watches through the leaves as the savages hold a ceremony at the sacred site marked by a great skull-shaped rock and a stone altar. As the boy watches, the savages drag a man onto the altar and sacrifice him. Later, after the savages have returned to their home island, the boy comes back with the girl and they find blood oozing down the side of the altar. The children never actually make contact with the savages. But the drumming and the human sacrifice clearly define the savages as sinister and mysterious. They are close to nature, to be sure, but in the American film nature is often dangerous for the children. These savages nicely fit the prototype of the Ignoble Savage.

The Indonesian version in most respects follows the American version closely—indeed, sometimes the shots are duplicated exactly. But the differences are significant. In Chapter 10 we shall compare the ways in which these same two films treat the individual in society. Here let us confine the discussion to the respective constructs of The (savage) Other. In the Indonesian film the boy and girl are captured by the tribe, pampered, worshiped as gods, and in the end escape.

These savages are dressed in quite primitive but nonrevealing clothing. The women wear elaborately sewn garments of banana leaves, the men furs and feathers and loincloths. We learn that their customs are on the whole disgusting. They smell so strongly that the young couple must cover their noses; the great feast they offer the couple is composed of inedible parts of inedible animals; their marriage ceremony consists of pouring sand over the principals; men get wives by pursuit and rape, watched approvingly by the tribal elders; and their language is composed of a few sounds which are identifiable as words and many sounds which are merely grunts and gurgles.

The reactions of the two young captives range from disgust to amusement. Twice they play tricks on the savages by working on their misguided beliefs that the two are gods. First, when the body stench is too bad, they invent a ritual dance which ends up as a group bath in the river; then, at a marriage ceremony, when they are brought to bless the bride and groom, they solemly spit in their faces, leading the entire tribe to file past and also spit in their faces. After each of these tricks—these ludicrous rituals—the captive couple laughs uproariously at the gullibility of the savages.

How do we make sense of this? If we refer to the two Western prototypes, these Indonesian cinema barbarians do fit the Ignoble Savage model better—mainly because they are certainly not Noble —but they are ludicrous and contemptible rather than fearsome. The two captives want to escape simply because they do not like being gods to the tribe, not because of any fear for their lives. Not surprisingly we must look for the origins of Indonesian constructs in Indonesia, not in the Western Wild Man.

For Indonesians the available prototype is not of a natural man, either noble or ignoble, but something that is more animal than human. In Europe, there was never any doubt about this human-sized furry creature. However degenerate, the Wild Man was a man. But it happens that the real world of the Indonesians holds a creature completely unknown to ancient and medieval Europe: a human-sized creature which lives in the jungle, is covered with fur, and is called *orang utan,* or "man of the forest." *Orang* is the common word for man, person, or human, but in this one compound it means not man but great ape. (And of course is one of the few Indonesian words used in English.)

The closeness of man to ape is suggested by an anecdote reported by Gregory Bateson:

> The late Doctor Stutterheim, Government Archeologist in Java, used to tell the following story: Somewhat before the advent of the white man, there was a storm on the Javanese coast in the neighborhood of one of the capitals. After the storm the people went down to the beach and found, washed up by the waves and almost dead, a white monkey of unknown species. The religious experts explained that this monkey had been a member of the court of Beroena, the God of the Sea, and that for some offense the monkey had been cast out by the god whose anger was expressed in the storm. The Rajah gave orders that the white monkey from the sea should be kept alive, chained to a certain stone. This was done. Doctor Stutterheim told me that he had seen the stone and that, roughly scratched on it in Latin, Dutch, and English, were the name of a man and a statement of his shipwreck. Apparently this trilingual sailor never established verbal communication with his captors. He was surely unaware of the premises in their minds which labelled him as a white monkey and therefore not a potential recipient of verbal messages: it probably never occurred to him that they could doubt his humanity. He may have doubted theirs. [1951:204 fn]

And of course "white monkey" suggests the figure of Hanuman in the Hindu *Ramayana* known to Indonesians in plays and puppet theater. Hanuman brings his monkey army to aid Rama in recapturing Sinta when she has been kidnapped. Hanuman is a favorite figure and although certainly not human, he has many human attributes. Moreover, the Loetoeng Kasaroeng, a West Javanese folktale, tells of the bewitched prince who turns into a great white ape.

We began by asking why the savages in the American *Blue Lagoon* are terrifying but in the Indonesian version merely ludicrous. The answer seems to lie in the differences between the cultural prototypes for savages available in each cultural tradition. For Westerners, savages are either Noble or they are dangerous barbarians. For Indonesians the prototype is of funny dumb animals. Of course, at a more thoughtful level Indonesians have no doubt that these tribes are human and, in fact, citizens of the republic. But the movies transport them back to the level of cultural stereotyping.

This, incidentally, helps to clarify a puzzle. When I show ethnographic films of the Dani, a tribal Papuan people of Irian Jaya (West New Guinea) to American undergraduates, they respond with serious interest. When I showed the same films to Indonesian undergraduates in my anthropology courses at Andalas University in West Sumatra, they roared with laughter. People will laugh for many different reasons, and it is extremely difficult to read such a complex utterance as laughter, especially the laughter of a group. But on the basis of the argument in this chapter I look at it this way: When I lectured on the Dani and asked exam questions about them, the Indonesian students responded seriously as I expected. But when the lights were out and the projector was running, they shifted into a sort of "movie mode" and saw the Dani as part of the ridiculous animal-like prototype in their popular culture.

As an even more speculative footnote it is worth considering Richard Bernheimer's suggestion that four different attitudes can be taken toward the Wild Man, "depending upon the degree of emotional detachment which the observer was able to achieve" (1952:4). They are, in order, fear, scornful laughter, interest, and, finally, admiration. Following Bernheimer's scheme, we see that the (fictional) Westerners in the Western films, who directly confront the savages, feel fear; the Indonesian characters and the Indonesian audiences, who are in fact immediate neighbors of such savages, laugh in scorn at them; but Western audiences, who are far removed from any possibility of actual encounter, feel intellectual curiosity.

In conclusion we see that Indonesian cinema in its genre films constructs the savage Other according to a prototype which resembles but is not the same as those of the West. And to emphasize that we are discussing prototypes in genre films, it can be mentioned that Teguh Karya, one of the most innovative of Indonesian cinematographic auteurs, in his film *Ibunda* (1986) presented a subtle complex picture of a young Papuan man in Java. The character was not a prototype—neither Noble Savage nor Ignoble Savage nor Great Ape—but a multidimensional personality.

CHAPTER 9

FEMINISM IN A MALE WORLD: CONTRADICTORY MESSAGES

What is the image of women in Indonesian films? Krishna Sen (1982) has concluded that they are portrayed as dependent and sinful. This view of the status of Indonesian women is widely held today. Yet the ethnographic descriptions of Indonesian culture suggest a much stronger, more positive, image of Indonesian women. And my own analysis of women in Indonesian films is closer to the ethnographies than to Sen's view. What is going on? Why is there so much variation? In this chapter we shall wade into the matter of feminism and film and try to sort things out. We shall find that many different, even contradictory, themes are being expressed in the portrayals of women in Indonesian cinema as well as in the roles of women in some of the peripheral cinema activities.

WOMEN IN ADVERTISING

Sen observes that film advertising "exploits the sexual and the exotic to sell goods" (1982:18). Actually, such exploitation is so widespread that it would be surprising only if it were not true in Indonesia. The movie ads and publications do portray women as sex objects. *Pos Film,* a weekly newspaper, has the crowded front-page layout typical of provincial Indonesian newspapers: a dozen or more articles, each with one or more photographs. Most of these photos are of women, some in provocative poses. *Majalah*

Film, which is more of a high-class biweekly (it costs Rp. 500 compared to *Pos Film* at Rp. 200) usually has one large photo and five smaller ones. The large picture is almost always of a female star. The smaller ones may include publicity shots of female or occasionally male stars, perhaps a production still or two from a film. Foreign stars and films may be featured in the smaller photographs.

Thus the emphasis is definitely on women: women as news, women as sales gimmicks. But women as sex objects? The general truth is that all such performers, male as well as female, are commodities—high-priced ones, to be sure, but commodities. Sen's argument is that women are offered more often than men, and women's sexuality is the prime attraction. As a generalization this seems to be true. But there are a couple of notes about the Indonesian-ness of film promotion worth making.

First, movie posters from *Majalah Film* show that the ads for Indonesian films are considerably less sexual than those for foreign films distributed in Indonesia. One can certainly see the use of women for the historical film and for the youth film but not for the comedy (Photos 1–3). Compare these three ads with two ads for Western films in the same magazine (Photos 11, 12), which are much more erotic. No Indonesian film ad could be so overtly sexy.

Second, two sorts of film promotion materials show a particularly Indonesian style: calendars and posters. Large wall calendars are sold in markets and on sidewalks during the last few months of each calendar year. The format is standard: There are six pages; the upper two-thirds of each page carries an illustration, usually a photograph; and across the bottom is the actual calendar for a pair of months. (In addition to the Julian calendar one usually finds also the Javanese, Chinese, and Muslim calendars.) One popular sort of calendar features color photographs of movie stars posing against generalized backgrounds. The stars are usually women, but they may be paired with a male star. The women's postures are demure, their costumes quite shapeless. Poses are strained—often the man has his hand resting uncomfortably on the woman's shoulder. If there is any hand-to-hand contact, it is not palm-to-palm. (See the discussion of this taboo in Chapter 5.)

The other sort of promotional materials are the light cardboard posters which are sold year-round in markets. Among the posters of soccer teams, Koranic scenes (Noah, Solomon), portraits of the president and vice-president (often with their families) one finds many posters of movie stars. Those of Western stars show, for example, Sylvester Stallone as Rambo, pectoral muscles glistening, or Farrah Fawcett in wet T-shirt. Posters of Indonesian stars, by contrast, resemble the calendar art but are even more constrained. In Photo 14 we see an especially domestic Yati Octavia, who actually plays fairly sexy parts. But here she is shown with her husband and their two small boys.

From a Western standpoint we would expect advertising to use more erotic images than actually appear in the films. And some movie advertising does. But there is also a trend in the opposite direction: situating these potentially sexy stars in more neutral, more familial, social relationships.

WOMEN IN FILM

On the whole the feminist criticism which Krishna Sen developed still holds. Indonesian cinema is a man's world. All aspects of the film industry—production, direction, criticism, in fact everything but acting—are in the hands of men. Women are at best peripheral.

And Sen's analysis of the ways in which women are depicted in movies is on the whole valid. Women are shown dependent on men, as being parts of social groups, while men can function independently—the career woman is an anomoly which must be resolved through domestication by the end of the film. There is a double standard in the portrayal of sexuality and its consequences: Women may enjoy sex only within the monogamous marriage, while men are allowed extramarital sex. And when women violate this rule of limited sexuality they vanish into the role of prostitute or die.

The 1988 film *Ayu Dan Ayu* (discussed in Chapter 4) exemplifies these principles. One Ayu is a physician but also the mother of two girls and the forgiving wife of the philandering man. The other Ayu, the Balinese dancer, is unmarried, has a career as a dancer, and has a son by the wandering husband. She violates both the norm of feminine dependency and the norm of limited sexuality. But she dies—thus giving a brilliant three-part solution to the plot. Not only does her death remove the double norm violations, but in dying she contributes her son to complete the family of the first Ayu and her (unchastened) husband. We are to understand that it was the lack of a son—that intolerable incompleteness—which had led the man to stray in the first place.

At first glance it is not surprising that women should be portrayed as passive and peripheral in Indonesian films. This is on the whole true of most Western films, and we do not doubt that Indonesian women are even less equal than Western women. Here we would be mistaken. Ethnographic reports and certain Indonesian movies present quite a different picture of the role of women.

WOMEN IN ETHNOGRAPHIES

There are a few Indonesian ethnographies which concern themselves directly with women. Hildred Geertz's study of the Javanese family depicts small-town domestic life in Central Java in the 1950s. About Javanese women she writes: "There is little of the man's world that they cannot participate in and still less that they do not know about" (1989:122). Although the bureaucracy is male, "in the sphere of everyday life, of getting and spending, women hold their own. Men, on the other hand, tend to be rather dependent—emotionally as well as practically—on women. . . . Javanese men rarely live alone, self-sufficient, whereas women frequently do" (1989:123). Geertz also writes that "the dimension of responsibility for major decisions of household management ranges from dominance by the wife to a point of almost complete equality between husband and wife, with discussion over every major decision. Rarely is a Javanese wife completely under the shadow of her husband, but there are many husbands who have passively surrendered to their wives" (1989:125).

Nancy Tanner has discussed "matrifocality" in three Indonesian cultures (1974)—drawing on Geertz's description of the Javanese family, her own research on Minangkabau of West Sumatra in the 1960s, and James Siegel's research on Aceh (1969). Tanner emphasizes the distinction between matrifocality and Anglo-American "momism," in which the woman, as a reaction to her extremely unequal economic and social role, creates a somewhat illegitimate form of control over her family. Matrifocality, on the other hand, is the sort of domestic arrangement in which the genders are relatively equal and where women have legitimate and respected economic and political power within the domestic group. Tanner recognizes this matrifocality in Java and in Aceh and especially in the matrilineal Minangkabau, which she knew firsthand.

There are several features of note about the various ethnographic reports which Tanner drew on. First, there seems to be a common Indonesian pattern emerging from cultures as diverse as Javanese, Aceh, and Minangkabau. Second, this pattern seems fairly traditional, for it has been identified primarily on the basis of data from town and village communities from the 1950s and 1960s—it is not merely a 1980s urban pattern. And third, it is a domestic pattern. These strong roles of women appear in the relatively egalitarian domestic setting, not in the admittedly male-dominated public sphere.

RESOLVING THE PARADOX

And this should give us a clue. For it is just in the Sentimental genre of film which plays out in the domestic arena that we find the independent woman. The official world—the world of bureaucracy and government, overwhelmingly a male preserve in Indonesia—comes into these domestic films only as incidental background or as setting for a scene which is essentially domestic. In fact, these domestic films play themselves out with a striking blindness to the male-oriented hierarchy which we know exists. There are scenes in all sorts of institutional settings—universities, hospitals, airport control towers, offices, sports leagues—in which we never see the Man In Charge. The plot is in each case focused on the domestic drama which has momentarily spilled out beyond the home. In one sense we can say that this is a technique of situating plot and players in the larger social context. But in fact it is done so sketchily and unrealistically that it hardly counts as sophisticated sociology. The outcome is that the Sentimental genre films play themselves out in that domestic arena where, according to the ethnographies, women are at least equal and often dominant.

We have already delineated (in Chapter 6) the Kartini prototype: a woman of middle age and traditional Indonesian beauty, usually in the background, who at a crucial moment in the plot intervenes to restore order or at least begin the process of restoring order. This Kartini figure is, in the flow of the plot, an extraordinary *dea ex machina*. But the central women—the wives, mothers, daughters, or fiancées in these domestic dramas—are strong independent women as well. And they play opposite males—husbands, fathers, sons, or fiancés—who are usually weak. The men are passive or, if active, create the disorder which must be salvaged in the end by the women.

This is the sort of generalized claim which can be illustrated by anecdote but is difficult to measure. Certainly there are exceptions —weak or foolish women—but they are far outnumbered by weak and foolish men. It is worth noting that two recent and celebrated films were entitled "Mother" (*Ibunda,* 1986) and "My Father" (*Ayahku,* 1988). Together they symbolize the point I am making. The first film was about a strong mother; the second concerned the absence and eventual return of an indifferent father. And although the pattern of strong women is particular to the Sentimental genre, it is not unknown elsewhere: The consensus Best Film of 1988, *Tjut Nya Dien,* is a historically accurate picture of the woman who led the Acehnese guerrilla forces against the Dutch for years around the turn of the century.

In short, women are portrayed in different and even contradictory ways in Indonesian cinema. But our expectations of finding that films exploit and oppress women must not blind us to the very strong image of women presented in some Indonesian films.

CHAPTER 10

INDIVIDUALS AND GROUPS: A MATTER OF EMPHASIS

It has been a basic assumption of this book that films, like any other sort of art, are rooted in their culture and shaped by its basic principles. It should follow, then, that if a film produced in one culture is remade in another, it is likely to be not simply translated but actually transformed in accordance with the principles of the second culture. Here, then, is the dual opportunity presented by these culture-crossing films: The changes are clues to cultural principles, and the cultural principles can explain the changes.

Translations of works from one language to another have always had a somewhat bad repute. If the translation is too faithful to the original, it is not itself an achievement; if it is too creative, it is unfaithful. Although in English we judge translation as a lover who is bound to be at least partially "unfaithful," the Italians use a stronger idiom playing on the similarity of *traditore* and *traduttore:* Translation is treason.

But if critics bemoan what is lost in translation, anthropologists can approach translation as transformation—and in that act of transformation find cultural principles. From this standpoint a work of literature, no matter how strongly shaped by the creative individual, is still rooted in the culture and provides grist for the anthropological mills. A provocative volume on translated plays edited by Hanna Scolnicov and Peter Holland sets out the possibilities of this sort of research: "The problem of the transference of plays from culture to culture is seen not just as a question of translating the text, but of conveying its meaning and adapting it to its new cultural environment so as to create new meanings" (1989:1). Despite these good intentions, the contributors to their volume do not really explore the implications of the "new cultural environment" beyond the odd interesting anecdote. For example: "The Yiddish playwright, Yakov Gordin, wrote *Mirele Ephos* (1898) as a kind of adaptation of *King Lear,* placing it in the context of the Jewish bourgeoisie of the late nineteenth century. The royal father's place was taken by the Yiddish mamme, Mirele Ephron, and, instead of Lear's three daughters, she has, of course, three sons" (1989:10).

Film scholars, also, have taken little advantage of the opportunities offered by transformed pairs of films. They generally see translation as degradation. Vincent Canby, writing in the *New York Times* (12 February 1989), deplores the trend toward American remakes of French films:

> Today [Hollywood] is swallowing up other countries' movies with a desperation unknown in the past, and never before to such muddled effect. . . . Most of these borrowings have been failures. Fabricated in Hollywood's mink-upholstered sweatshops, they emerge looking like stateless reproductions . . .
>
> Each film, in its witless way, helps to define the differences between American films and those from abroad. These are differences to be appreciated as much as whales and rain forests.
>
> They need to be protected if movies aren't eventually to evolve their own uninational character, as interchangeable as chain hotels from New York to London, Paris, Cairo and Tokyo.

But there is an alternative to thinking in Canby's terms about "stateless reproductions": the possibility that we can see these American remakes of French films as American films in which the French principles have been changed into American principles. And, in this case, we have a basis for understanding the change. It is the 1950 book *Movies* by Martha Wolfenstein and Nathan Leites, which was based on a study of American, English, and French films of the late 1940s. Wolfenstein and Leites have spelled out the ways in which various motifs and themes differ in each of the three national cinemas. From their book one can draw a set of postulates or predictions about different plot motifs and apply it to a pair of translated/transformed films.

COUSINS AND COUSINS

Cousins, an American film released in 1989, is a remake of the 1976 French film *Cousin, Cousine.* The American version has exactly reproduced many particulars of the French original, both major and minor. Both films are relentlessly family oriented. This is expected of French but not of American films. ("American films tend to picture both hero and heroine unbound by family ties. . . . French films provide the hero and heroine with family relations more frequently. . . . The French show the woman as more family-bound than the man," note Wolfenstein and Leites 1950:101, 102.)

The American film presents a family setting hedged in a manner typical of such films: It is strongly ethnic European—the hero's family is very Polish, hers very Italian; in fact, the heroine is played by Isabella Rosselini, herself famously Swedish-Italian. In reality, of course, Americans of British stock have families, too, but the literary/film convention is to show hero and heroine as without family ties. Thus family films are specially marked by being set in the Deep South or in immigrant southern or eastern European contexts. (*Moonstruck* is the Italian Bronx of the 1980s; Leonard Bernstein used Puerto Rican New York for his *West Side Story* transformation of *Romeo and Juliet*—neither could have been set in contemporary Kansas.)

But the strongest evidence for the different culture patterns is in the structure of love shown in the two films. According to Wolfenstein and Leites, certain principles of romance govern American films: Lovers may part but they do get a second chance; no one can be really in love with more than one person; love never runs down; and love rarely involves suffering or ends unhappily. In French films, however, lovers never get a second chance, one can fall out of love with one partner and into love with another, and love often involves suffering or ends unhappily (1950:24, 92, 98, 99).

The plots of *Cousin, Cousine* and *Cousins* are essentially the same: Two married couples are brought into cousinlike relationship by the marriage of the hero's uncle to the heroine's mother. Gradually hero and heroine are attracted to each other, encourage their respective philandering spouses to believe they are having an affair, eventually do, and then in the end go off together. But in two respects the films handle the shift of love quite differently. In the French version the original coupling fades into indifference as the hero and heroine develop their relationship. In the American version the original couples try to resume their relationships with their spouses, time passes, but eventually the reconciliations fail and the new lovers come together again. In the French version the original couples get no such second chance.

The French version involves much suffering all around: The hero's wife has a series of mental breakdowns; the heroine's husband takes to drink; the hero and heroine enjoy arousing suspicions (which are at first unjust) and later confirming them and in the end abruptly walking out together at a family Christmas party. But in the American version no one really suffers and early on the heroine takes great pains to assure her rival that they are just pretending to have an affair to get revenge for themselves being betrayed. The hero's wife, after separation, becomes a happy and successful businesswoman, the heroine's husband himself offers to leave her, and in the end the hero and heroine, with his son and her daughter, happily sail off in their little boat together.

Cousins has been transformed not just by its North American setting and its 1980s artifacts but by a partial accommodation to some of those American patterns which had been recognized by Wolfenstein and Leites in the 1940s. This sort of analysis depends not only on the availability of a pair of films but also on some understanding of relevant cultural differences. Wolfenstein and Leites' study is a model of comparisons within three sets of national films, American, French, and English. Although it systematically lays out differences, in the end it makes only cursory efforts to tie them to more pervasive cultural differences.

Here, as we turn to Indonesian films and search for basic cultural differences, we find a particularly useful cultural diagnostic: a position along a continuum which I have called the individual/social interaction. To recapitulate my observations in Chapter 3: Cultures differ greatly in the degree to which they emphasize the self as an autonomous individual or as a member of a social group or network. It is dangerous to simplify this idea into an opposition between "individualistic" cultures and "social" cultures, for we are dealing with relative emphases along a continuum. Thus, as we

have seen, Wolfenstein and Leites conclude that in their films the French emphasize family groups while the Americans emphasize individuals apart from their families.

There is strong evidence that in many areas of culture, Indonesians tend to emphasize social groups whereas Americans tend to emphasize autonomous, ostensibly unattached, individuals. (A handy diagnostic question: Who makes marriage arrangements? In America this is ideally a purely individual decision in which the families have no say; in many parts of Indonesia it is the family groups which make the arrangements on behalf of the individuals.) In cinema this difference becomes especially apparent when American films are translated and transformed into Indonesian films.

BLUE AND NOT SO BLUE LAGOONS

One such pair of films is *Blue Lagoon* (1980; starring Brooke Shields) and *Pengantin Pantai Biru* (The Bride of the Blue Shore), written and directed by Wim Umboh and starring Meriam Bellina and Sandro Tobing. The story is the same in both films: Two children, together with a man, are cast ashore on a deserted tropical coast. The man teaches the children basic survival skills before he dies. The children reach adolescence and discover adulthood, love, and sexuality on their own. They encounter a savage tribe, but escape. They have a baby and are finally rescued by the hero's father, who has been searching for them all the while.

We have already examined this pair of films in Chapter 8 in discussing how films construct the culture of The Other. Now we can return to the pair for another illustration. The American version of the plot is situated at the extreme "individual" end of the spectrum. It would be hard to imagine more individual autonomy than this—well, perhaps Robinson Crusoe would be more extreme. But here we have two children cut off from their society. Even the old man, when he has imparted his knowledge to them, is superfluous and disappears from the scene. There is a social group in the vicinity, but it is the threatening savage. And then, just when they are rescued and about to be returned to their social network, the movie ends.

It would be hard to imagine a less Indonesian story. It was

surely the sexuality of the plot, not the isolation of the principals, which attracted the Indonesian filmmakers. On the whole, *Pengantin Pantai Biru* is a literal, "faithful," translation of *Blue Lagoon*. But here we are interested in those points on which the films differ, for in this we shall see how the Indonesian version, while remaining basically faithful to the American version, has shifted systematically and somewhat akwardly toward greater social embeddedness.

This shift is apparent in several particulars. In the American version the older man cast ashore with the two children is just a lower-class cook (Leo McKern, of *Rumpole* fame). In the Indonesian version he is the little girl's father. The class consciousness of the American version, often played for laughs in the film, is replaced in the Indonesian version by a family tie.

Moreover, there is a savage tribe living on a distant part of the island (or perhaps it just visits the island for blood ceremonies). The castaways often hear drumming. In the American version the savages are mainly unseen boogeymen. The children have no direct contact with them, and only once does the boy actually catch a glimpse of them as he spies on a human sacrifice ceremony. In the Indonesian version the children—already adolescents—are more or less captured by the savages, held against their will, fed, and worshiped as gods. They are not willing gods, and they do eventually escape, but they have spent much of the film in a broader social context of sorts.

In the American film the young couple twice see a ship. Each time they decide not to declare themselves, choosing to remain in their social isolation. In the end they and their child accidentally drift out to sea in their oarless dinghy and float for days. When the ship does finally come to the rescue, all three are unconscious. They have done their best to shun their own society, and the emotional tone of the reunion between the hero and his father is left to our imagination. In the Indonesian version, the ship searching for them appears five times. Each time the castaways try in vain to signal, until the fifth time when they are rescued and we see the joyous reunion between father and son. For the American couple this reclusive state is ideal; for the Indonesian couple it is to be abandoned as quickly as possible.

There are other differences. For example, in the American version there is explicit class structure as well as quite explicit sexual-

ity, including masturbation and nudity. In the American version
the two seem to invent sexual intercourse by themselves, while the
Indonesian couple apparently learn from seeing rape among the
savages. In both versions nature has its beautiful moments, but
only in the American version is it also constantly dangerous: There
are poison berries, deadly spiked rockfish, sharks, scorpions. For
the Americans the savages are sinister with their human sacrifices;
for the Indonesians the savages are ridiculous, contemptible, and
smelly.

But most significant is the way that the Indonesian film has
managed to socialize the couple despite the entire logic of the plot.
It has been profoundly Indonesianized. Viewed in these terms,
also, we see Indonesian cinema becoming more Indonesian in the
face of strong foreign influence, especially from America. In some
respects—the most obvious being sexuality—Indonesian cinema is
indeed becoming more Americanized: Lip-to-lip kissing, palm-to-
palm hand holding, and revealing clothing are, by the late 1980s,
allowed in Indonesian films. Perhaps what is most remarkable is
not that a film about youthful sexuality like *Pengantin Pantai Biru*
is now able to be made in Indonesia but that this film and other
recent Indonesian efforts show with such robustness the imprint
of basic Indonesian patterns. At the deepest levels, Indonesian
film is becoming more Indonesian.

LONG MARCHES REVISITED

Looking at many of the earliest extant Indonesian films, those
from the 1950s, I find it remarkable that they are individual-ori-
ented, not group-oriented. If we return to the contrast between
Darah Dan Do'a (1950) and *Mereka Kembali* (1973), discussed in
Chapter 7, we see this point clearly. Even though *Darah Dan Do'a*
is subtitled "The Long March," the fate of the individual officer
Sudarto is more important than that of the Siliwangi Division.
Midway through the film, Sudarto leaves the Long March and
goes into a nearby town in search of medical supplies for the
wounded. This in itself is significant. In *Mereka Kembali* the
wounded do not divert the army from its mission. In fact, one
badly wounded man is sacrificed for the good of the group: He is
left behind, back against a tree, with gun and ammunition to hold

off the Dutch pursuers until his comrades can make their escape. There is a subplot concern with medicine in *Mereka Kembali,* but it is civilians who bring it to the troops—officers do not leave their command to get it.

But in *Darah Dan Do'a* Sudarto not only goes into town for supplies—he visits a woman, is captured by the Dutch, and is thrown into prison. The movie now abandons the Siliwangi Division and follows Sudarto to his lonely death, the act of individual revenge. And as he is shot in his study, he is reading over his wartime diary. We have seen him writing in it from time to time. Once he began a sentence, "I feel . . . ," and then crossed it out. And at one point he actually says, "Sometimes I don't understand the Struggle." Such rampant individualism in details large and small does not figure in the 1975 version. There everything is directed toward the group. Soldiers live and die for the army. Even the young newly married couple—both soldiers—die together in a Darul Islam ambush, their bloody fingers touching. There is good-natured grumbling on the part of the heroic sergeant but no serious questioning of the meaning of the Struggle. There is much emphasis on the division's motto—Esa Hilang, Dua Terbilang (When One Falls, Two Rise Up)—and on its sacred flag, which must be protected from Darul Islam at all costs.

Final scenes always beg for special attention. In *Darah Dan Do'a* the last shot is of the Siliwangi officer, alone in his room, rolling dead on the floor, killed by an act of private revenge. In *Mereka Kembali* the final scene depicts the burial of the heroic sergeant, killed fighting the Darul Islam forces, and the camera tilts from his grave upward to the two flags, the *puji* of Siliwangi and the Red and White of the republic, against the sky, with the division's motto printed across the frame.

Here we see a shift in Indonesian filmmaking from the 1950s to the 1970s. Interestingly the two directors were of the same generation (see Sinematek Indonesia 1979): Usmar Ismail was born in 1921, Nawi Ismail in 1918; both were educated in Dutch schools (HIS and MULO), both worked on films during the Japanese occupation, and both became active in Indonesian films from 1950 on. Clearly, then, this shift in filmmaking is not so much an individual effect as one of changing film culture. In terms of the individual/social dimension, we can see the period immediately after independence as one when Indonesian creativity was still

strongly influenced by Dutch and European principles. Only later
do we see a movement away from them, an Indonesianization of
the national cinema.

Other early films have messages of individualism similar to that
of *Darah Dan Do'a: Lewat Djam Malam* (After the Curfew) is
about a disillusioned veteran of the revolution who refuses to join
in the corruption of his former comrades in arms and in the end is
destroyed by them. *Pagar Kawat Berduri* (Barbed Wire) by Asrul
Sani is a fairly late example (1961) but one of the best. The guerrilla leader, captured by the Dutch, has long talks with the sympathetic Dutch major, the commandant of the prison. They play
chess and debate the meaning of life and war. In the end the major
shoots himself out of despair and the guerrilla is led away to a fir-
ing squad. This plot is reminiscent of Renoir's *Grand Illusion,* a
strong picture of individuals grappling with the unbearable while
the great events of armies and nations swirl around them. *Pedjuang* (The Freedom Fighter), also by Usmar Ismail, is about a
rollicking boisterous soldier. There is much concern with individuals—when one man is wounded, a tremendous debate rages over
the relative importance of The Individual and The Struggle. In the
end they do leave him to fall into Dutch hands, but later there is
another argument over whether or not they should rescue him
from the Dutch. Eventually they do—at great cost.

This individualism which marks the earlier films is very rare in
the later ones. One could call the later pattern more "patriotic,"
but this is misleading. Much of the behavior in earlier films is
quite patriotic, or at least not unpatriotic, for people are still
working for the revolution. It makes more sense to describe it in
terms of the individual/group continuum: The first Indonesian
films were more individualistic, the later ones more group-oriented. But this brings us up against a paradox: To the extent that
Indonesian culture in general and in its regional particulars has
changed along this continuum at all, it has moved toward more
individualism since 1950. People are less constrained by family
and clan demands, they are more willing to move to other regions,
to choose their own marriage partners, and to marry outside their
own ethnic groups. Yet the films made in Indonesia have evolved
in the opposite direction since 1950. In fact, it looks rather more
like a convergence in culture and film—the culture becoming less
traditional, the film more traditional.

And there lies the surprise. But of course the first decade of Indonesian films, in the 1950s, was still under the strong influence of the Western individualistic tradition propagated by the Dutch. The filmmakers of the 1950s, men like Usmar Ismail, Djajaku-suma, and Asrul Sani, had gone through Dutch schools, studied European literature, and often studied in the West (Ismail at the University of Southern California, Sani at UCLA and in the Netherlands). Their films dealt with Indonesian subjects in Western, individualistic ways. Later, as the film industry evolved in the hands of a younger generation, there were several reasons why the films became more Indonesian: Although these young filmmakers were not thinking in the explicit anthropological terms used in this book, they were still looking more consciously to forge an Indonesian identity in cinema. Later directors visited abroad (Teguh Karya in Hawaii, Syumandjaya in Moscow), but these men were born in the mid-1930s, too late to experience the full Dutch educational treatment.

When introducing the concepts of genre and auteur films in Chapter 1, I remarked that auteur films, even though they avoided the genre formulas, had to be rooted in their culture to some extent. For evidence of this we can return to *Doea Tanda Mata,* the much-acclaimed film by Teguh Karya about the nationalistic movement during the 1930s. It is a story of tension between individual and group. Goenadi is pulled by two groups: One is his wife and her fellow nationalists in the village; the second is the men who work the printing press in Bandung. He leaves the village for the city group; he then leaves the city group to pursue his infatuation with Miss Ining, the Teater Stambul singer. He fails in both respects, for he does not achieve the essentially asocial union with Miss Ining and he is not reincorporated into either group. He succeeds only in the intensely personal act of revenge, jealousy, and self-justification, shooting the Dutch officer. But in the end he is killed in a way reminiscent of the ending of *Darah Dan Do'a,* where the hero is killed and dies a solitary death. And after Goenadi's death, there is an interesting coda in which his widow reads aloud his last letter, thus allowing Goenadi to comment on his own fate. The final words of the film show his belated realization: "I have too much ambition but too little ability. The result is only foolishness heaped on foolishness." (. . . terlalu besar keinginannya tapi terlalu kecil kemampuannya. Dan buahnya

sekarang ini hanyalah kekonyolan demi kekonyolan.) (This ending also recalls that of *The Bridge on the River Kwai.*)

Doea Tanda Mata is both an auteur film and an unmistakably
Indonesian film. In its structure it recalls the Indonesian tradition;
in its themes it plays with the tension between individual and
group, even as it comes to an untraditional conclusion; and it is at
its most original in avoiding conventional Indonesian narrative
motifs. So the paradox is rephrased as a dynamic tension: In some
respects Indonesian culture is becoming more like that of the
West; Indonesian films are in many ways being influenced by
Western, and especially by American, films; but in terms of these
fundamental cultural premises, Indonesian films have become
more Indonesian since 1950.

CHAPTER 11

NATIONAL CINEMA, NATIONAL CULTURE

From the beginning of this book I have made a somewhat artificial distinction between film as the passive reflection of culture and film as the active agent of change. This has been a useful analytic device as far as it goes, but in fact just as auteur films may draw on elements from genre films, the same film may have both active and the passive functions.

A film which provides a clear example of this dual active and passive role of cinema and also makes a significant political statement is *Puteri Giok* (The Jade Princess) (1981). *Puteri Giok* is at once a formulaic Sentimental youth film reflecting many of the Indonesian features which we have discussed, and a blatant propaganda piece pushing the case for cultural assimilation under the New Order ideology. It is especially interesting because it is one of the only Indonesian films to treat Indonesian Chinese in anything like a realistic manner. If they appear at all in films, Indonesian Chinese have minor and usually negative stereotyped roles: greedy money lender (in *Nyai Dasima*), procurer (in *Salah Asuhan*), con man (in *Desa Di Kaki Bukit*), pickpocket (in *Raja Copet*), or, for a change, token soldier (in *Mereka Kembali*). But in *Puteri Giok* the Chinese family is at the center of the action and their Chinese status is the basis of the plot.

The film does not fit easily into any of the standard Indonesian cinematic genres. It could be described as a New Order patriotic Sentimental High School film. At first it seems to be a social problem film since it deals with relations between majority and minority ethnic groups, but in fact it delicately avoids any indication that the minority is discriminated against. The only recognizable obstacles to assimilation are the Chinese father and his business associates, and by the end of the film even they have seen the light and enthusiastically accept assimilation. What makes it a social problem film, then, is not any sort of insightful analysis or depiction of a social problem, but rather the oblique allusion to a problem of minority discrimination.

The Western "social problem film" is one which deals in an obvious and didactic way with a social problem, pitting an individual against social institutions (see Roffman and Purdy 1981). This film neatly sidesteps the problem, but it offers a solution. From the first scene to the last we are in no doubt that the solution lies in assimilation through the moral charter of the Indonesian state, the Pancasila (the Five Principles). This is a patriotic political film par excellence (Berita Minggu Film of 2 November 1981, p. 8, used the phrase "bernafas P4"—it smells like a primer on the Pancasila). Problems are usually more interesting than solutions, so most films concentrate on the confusion and destruction of an expanding problem. Perhaps in this instance, because the problem is both so well known and so politically sensitive, we are presented with ninety minutes of solution.

As we have seen again and again, Indonesian cinema is a powerful vehicle for the development, shaping, and diffusion of a national Indonesian culture. Films employ a few standard indices of regional languages and cultures, but only to signify that all those people who participate in the national culture are in some fairly inconsequential way Batak or Balinese or whatever.

The opening scene of *Puteri Giok* epitomizes this: The camera pans across a great chorus of people wearing the special dress of each Indonesian ethnic group or province. But they are all behaving the same, singing the Indonesian patriotic anthem in harmony. The regional costumes serve only to show that wherever they come from, the singers have now joined in a single nationalistic chorus: Out of Many, One (the Indonesian national motto).

This flattening of the ethnic specifics extends, curiously enough, even to the Han family, which is only symbolically Chinese. Of course, we do not expect ethnographic precision in a feature film, but it is hard to identify any behavior or artifact which differentiates this family from any other upper-class Jakarta family pictured in the Sentimental family films produced over the last two decades in Indonesia. I see only two markers of their ethnicity: The mother lights joss sticks and prays before a figure of the Buddha, and a vertical Chinese painting hangs on the wall (nicely contrasting with the prototypical horizontal mountain-and-water Indonesian landscape hanging in the family house of Herman, Giok Nio's Indonesian boyfriend).

Religion—an important constituent of the national culture—cannot be generalized or standardized, so in these sorts of films, religions are made interchangeable. In fact, this movie takes it to extremes: Giok Nio (the "Jade Princess") is Catholic, her mother is Buddhist, and her brother is Muslim. In an interesting plot move, Giok is the star of a champion women's softball team, which seems like another extreme instance of this construction of a new Indonesian national culture. To be sure, there are softball teams in Indonesia. Prambors, Giok's team, is an actual team, and some of the players may have bit parts in the film. But of all the extracurricular activities available to a high school girl in Indonesia, softball is one of the most unusual.

But softball, or even the Indonesian language, is not cast as the vehicle of Indonesian unity. It is patriotism, harkening back to the Struggle for independence and expressed in the Pancasila, that will unite all the peoples into a single chorus. The Struggle is alluded to in the school pageant in which Giok Nio plays the lead, dressed as a sort of Spirit of Indonesia, Joan of Arc, and Goddess of Liberty, holding aloft a *kris,* the sacred mystical knife of Indonesia.

The Pancasila is evoked by the teacher's lecture to Giok's high school class from the textbook *Pendidikan Moral Pancasila* in the second scene of the film, immediately following the chorus. It is employed even more pointedly by Giok's brother, Tek Liong, as he goes to confront Wijay, the troublemaker. Wijay is a slick operator, the real estate developer and partner of their father. He has on his office wall the obligatory photographs of the president and the vice-president flanking the large plaque of the garuda holding the shield with symbols for each of the Five Principles. But Wijay is definitely non-Indonesian. Ethnically he is South Asian (and is played by an actor from Pakistan). He expresses scorn for Indonesia and he peppers his talk with the English pronouns "I" and "you." But Tek Liong gives him a mesmerizing lecture on the Pancasila and after he stalks out of the office, Wijay stares at the wall plaque as the words and songs ring in his mind.

In an obvious way, this film champions social change, and the moral intent of the film is to encourage assimilation of all peoples

in Indonesia. There have been few Indonesian films with so
explicit a message. To be sure, Perjuangan films celebrate heroism
in the revolution, many films advertise tourist spots, and a film
like *Desa Di Kaki Bukit* touts the virtues of family planning. But
as one reviewer wrote, *Puteri Giok* has the "bau-bau sponsor"
(the odor of a sponsor).

The classic Indonesian plot, described in Chapter 4, is clearly
recognizable. The major twist which *Puteri Giok* gives to the prototype is to focus on Giok's softball team, not her family, as the
prime social group. This group is disrupted through the innuendos
whispered to Giok's father by the agent of disorder, Wijay. Liong
Swei shaves his daughter's head and forbids her to play in the
championship game. After losing the game, the team members
storm over to Giok's house searching for her. There are actually
three reunions: one with the team members at Giok's bedside, a
second with all the survivors at the joint gravesides of Giok and
Herman (the unhappy ending) and the third reunion with everyone
at the engagement party (the happy ending). The status of the two
alternative endings is ambiguous, but perhaps the first, unhappy,
ending is meant to be a dream of the father's which converts him
to acceptance of assimilation.

The important Indonesian theme of the primacy of the group
over the individual runs throughout *Puteri Giok*. Liong Swei, the
father, breaks up his son's relationship with Indrawati (an Indonesian girl) and Giok's relationship with the team and with Herman.
Although both children resent his authority, they bend to it with
little rebellion. Tek Liong accepts his father's dismissal of Indrawati, and it is actually she who explains that parents know best. As
he shaves her head, Liong Swei blames Giok not for sinning, but
for embarrassing the family. And in the final scene neither couple
is reunited until Liong himself sanctions it by physically bringing
them together. The film is not so much about youth rebelling and
finding themselves—that would be the American version. It is
about youth accepting the authority of the family and being sty-
mied until the father changes his mind.

We also see the second basic theme of Indonesian films, that of
order vs. disorder, where the opening order is disrupted by an
agent of disorder, but at the end order is reinstated. Tek Liong
realizes this clearly and bemoans the confusion and disorder
(using, at different times, the words *kacau* and *kalap*), identifying

Wijay as the person who created disorder *(menghasut)*. The telling difference between this theme and the western theme of good vs. evil is that the bad guy is punished, but the agent of disorder is reincorporated into the group. Wijay is an examplary agent of disorder (a *penghasut,* or agitator). There is a second condensed version of the same progression from order through disorder and back to order again in the high school pageant. It opens with posed soldiers of the revolution singing a patriotic song, and the atmosphere gradually intensifies, cutting to stock shots of modern jet fighters flying by, then superimposing the military display footage over the school production. As the sound and visuals grow denser, the camera rocks on its tripod, making the horizontal axis tilt wildly. Then, at the height of this confusion, order is suddenly restored by the triumphant appearance of Giok as the goddess.

Narrative conventions of Indonesian formula films, described in Chapter 5, are also evident, although *Puteri Giok* does employ some unusual ones. The scene in which Liong Swei shaves his daughter's head is the most dramatic and emotional one of the entire film. But where does this head-shaving come from? In other Indonesian films, long, loose hair is worn by women who are mad or sexually promiscuous (that is, in some state of disorder). Liong is punishing his daughter for what he sees as sexual misconduct (although what he says is that she has made her family ashamed— *malu*). So the shaving is understandable as an act removing the outward sign of disorder, but it is certainly not a common motif in Indonesia. One can find it elsewhere, though. At the end of World War II Frenchwomen who had consorted with German occupiers had their heads shaved. And Provencher (1971:135) reported that Malays in Kuala Lumpur commonly shaved the heads of thieves or those who had committed sexual sins (fornication or adultery).

A second unexpected motif is the double suicide of Giok and Herman, who jump down the waterfall in the unhappy ending. William Frederick describes an Indonesian film of the Japanese Period *(Kali Seraya)* with the same double suicide, and he calls it a "recognizably Japanese—and thoroughly un-Indonesian resolution" (1989:130, n. 177). It is certainly not a standard Indonesian motif, and in fact suicide of any sort is rare in Indonesian films (I cannot think of any other examples).

In the key scene of the physical punishment—shaving the head —of the daughter by the father, the act is feebly resisted by the

mother. Physical violence is extremely rare in any Indonesian films
except for the violent genres like war films, horror films, and colonial films. But when it does occur in the Sentimental films it is
invariably violence directed against children, usually on the part
of the parents, and is often the result of misunderstanding, not
actual transgressions by the child.

A common premonition of disaster in Indonesian movies is the
breaking of a mirror, drinking glass, pot, or the like. Given the
frequency of this motif, it seems likely that when Herman smashes
the glass table top in his rampage just before the double suicide,
Indonesian audiences are signaled that tragedy is about to occur.

Although this film is about youthful sexuality, real and imag-
ined, it is seldom actually depicted. (Since this film was made in
1981, sexuality has become much more explicit in many Indonesian films.) One of the most Indonesian restrictions—that lovers
never hold hands with palm-to-palm contact—is especially evident
in the sequences when Herman and Giok run away to commit suicide. They go to extraordinary lengths *not* to make palm-to-palm
contact.

So we have a social problem film that is all solution, no problem. We have a film about Indonesian Chinese that is all Indonesian, with no real ethnic element. This says much about the role of
Indonesian Chinese in modern Indonesian life. And it especially
speaks to the complex role which movies play in the development
of a national Indonesian culture, a melting pot in which all are to
be assimilated, with only a few remaining markers to remind one
of the original cultural ingredients.

Thus *Puteri Giok* exemplifies the way in which Indonesian films
are rooted in Indonesian culture and yet promote changes in Indonesian life. The messages of these films are varied indeed, and few
films are quite as blatant about pushing changes as *Puteri Giok*.
But the more closely we look at Indonesian films, the more clearly
we see that one of the most powerful messages concerns this
national Indonesian culture.

In this cultural analysis I have taken a variety of approaches to
Indonesian cinema—each based on the assumption that films are
part of the larger cultural picture. I have slighted the history of
Indonesian films in the expectation that English-speaking readers
should soon have access to Salim Said's excellent study of the subject. And Krishna Sen should soon publish her more intensely

political analysis of Indonesian films. Eventually, perhaps, we can even hope for a close cinematographic reading of Indonesian films along the lines which Donald Richie, David Bordwell, and others have laid out for Japanese film. But this is a cultural analysis, and the conclusions properly lead us to a deeper understanding of Indonesian culture. And, in fact, it is fair to say that we see some things more clearly through a study of films than we do through traditional studies.

First, of course, because films are a manifestation of cultural principles at the national level, we are able to see "culture" at the national level—that is, "Indonesian culture"—in a way not possible when we observe village or city life. There, on the ground, one sees the regional culture mixed with the national culture. We are used to this in language. In Bukittinggi, for example, people switch back and forth between the regional language, Minangkabau, and a Minangkabau-influenced version of the national language, Indonesian. Yet there is also a nonregional standard Indonesian which is taught at home and abroad and represented in grammars, dictionaries, fiction, and nonfiction. It is quite permissible to speak of a "standard" nonregional Indonesian even though most people actually speak it with a strong regional flavor.

But the rest of culture generally runs deeper than language. We are not so aware of it, and its rules are not laid out in textbooks and taught systematically in schools. No one has ever taken an oath to follow standard Indonesian cultural rules in the way that the students vowed to use the Indonesian language at a conference on 28 October 1928. Then, in their famous Youth Pledge, they proclaimed one land, one people, and one language, but *not* one culture (Anwar 1980:15).

This omission of Indonesian culture per se was more understandable in 1928 when, for tactical reasons, the emphasis was on language alone. But now a national culture does exist, in an emerging form at least, and it is most clearly visible as a fictional construct in Indonesian films. There are other national vehicles of cultural patterns: magazines, newspapers, novels, and the single television channel which reaches into every part of the archipelago. But the films, and especially the domestic Sentimental genre films, can present a particularly well-rounded and accessible picture of the emergent national culture.

There are several features of Indonesian culture which are particularly evident in these films, and which account for much of the exoticness perceived by non-Indonesian viewers (especially Westerners). We have explored them repeatedly throughout this book: The theme of social embeddedness—as opposed to a Western emphasis on individual autonomy—runs through many of these Indonesian films. The theme of order and disorder—as opposed to a Western emphasis on good and evil—motivates the plot line in these films. In some of the more obvious and superficial respects Indonesian films are certainly becoming more Western, or perhaps more international. But there is good reason to think that in the modern period, say 1950 to the present, they are actually becoming more Indonesian in terms of their deeper features. The films are increasingly concerned with the specifically Indonesian shape of modernization and development, they are more often retelling the stories of Indonesian history and legend, and above all they are more involved in working out these particularly Indonesian cultural themes as they construct a national culture.

BIBLIOGRAPHY

Allan, Jeremy
  1985   "Review of Doea Tanda Mata." *Jakarta Post,* 12 October 1985.

Anderson, Benedict R. O'G.
  1965   *Mythology and the Tolerance of the Javanese.* Monograph Series, Modern Indonesian Project. Ithaca: Cornell University, Southeast Asia Program.

  1978   "Cartoons and Monuments: The Evolution of Political Communication Under the New Order." In Karl D. Jackson and Lucian W. Pye (eds.), *Political Power and Communications in Indonesia.* Berkeley: University of California Press.

Anderson, David Charles
  1976   "The Military Aspects of the Madiun Affair." *Indonesia* 21:1–63.

Anwar, Khaidir
  1980   *Indonesian: The Development and Use of a National Language.* Yogyakarta: Gadjah Mada University Press.

Archipel
  1973   "Le Cinema Indonesien." *Archipel* 5:51–250.

Ardan, S. M.
  1984   "Bioskop dalam Sejarah Perfilman di Indonesia." In *Data Perbioskopan di Indonesia 1984.* Jakarta: Department Penerangan R.I.

  1985   "In Memoriam: Sjuman Djaya (1934–1985)." *Indonesia* 40:122–126.

Bachtiar, Harsya W.
  1985   "Konsensus dan Konflik dalam Sistem Budaya di Indonesia." In *Budaya Dan Manusia Indonesia.* Yogyakarta: YP2LPM.

Balai Pustaka
  1964   *National Culture and Education: Planned Overall Pattern of National Development.* Translated by A. P. Crow. Jakarta: n.p.

Bateson, Gregory
  1951   "Information and Codificiation: A Philosophical Approach." In Jurgen Ruesch and Gregory Bateson (eds.), *Communication: The Social Matrix of Psychiatry.* New York: W. W. Norton.

Becker, A. L.
  1979   "Text-Building, Epistemology, and Aesthetics in Javanese Shadow Theatre." In A. L. Becker and Aram A. Yengoyan (eds.), *The Imagination of Reality: Essays in Southeast Asian Coherence Systems.* Norwood, N.J.: Ablex.

Becker, Judith
  1979 "People Who Sing: People Who Dance." In Gloria Davis (ed.), *What Is Modern Indonesian Culture?* Athens: Center for International Studies, Ohio University.

Beeman, William O.
  1986 *Language, Status, and Power in Iran.* Bloomington: Indiana University Press.

Benedict, Ruth
  1934 *Patterns of Culture.* Boston: Houghton Mifflin.

  1946 *The Chrysanthemum and the Sword: Patterns of Japanese Culture.* Boston: Houghton Mifflin.

Bernheimer, Richard
  1952 *Wild Men in the Middle Ages: A Study in Art, Sentiment, and Demonology.* Cambridge: Harvard University Press.

Bordwell, David
  1988 *Ozu and the Poetics of Cinema.* Princeton: Princeton University Press.

  1989 *Making Meaning: Inference and Rhetoric in the Interpretation of Cinema.* Cambridge: Harvard University Press.

Bordwell, David, Janet Staiger, and Kristin Thompson
  1985 *The Classical Hollywood Cinema: Film Style and Mode of Production to 1960.* New York: Columbia University Press.

Brandon, James R.
  1970 *On Thrones of Gold: Three Javanese Shadow Plays.* Cambridge: Harvard University Press.

Bruner, Edward M.
  1961 "Urbanization and Ethnic Identity in North Sumatra." *American Anthropologist* 63:508–521.

  1979 "Comments: Modern? Indonesian? Culture?" In Gloria Davis (ed.), *What Is Modern Indonesian Culture?* Athens: Center for International Studies, Ohio University.

Caldarola, Victor J.
  1989 "Medium Reception and Muslim Orthodoxy in Outer Indonesia." Paper presented at the Annual Meetings of the American Anthropological Association in Washington, D.C.

Collier, John, and Malcolm Collier
  1987 *Visual Anthropology.* 2d ed. Albuquerque: University of New Mexico Press.

Danandjaja, James
  1984 *Folklor Indonesia.* Jakarta: Grafitipers.

Doherty, Thomas
  1988 *Teenagers and Teenpics: The Juvenilization of American Movies in the 1950s.* Boston: Unwin Hyman.

Drake, Christine
1989   *National Integration in Indonesia: Patterns and Policies.* Honolulu: University of Hawaii Press.

Dundes, Alan
1965   *The Study of Folklore.* Englewood Cliffs, N.J.: Prentice-Hall.

Edwards, Walter
1989   *Modern Japan Through Its Weddings: Gender, Person, and Society in Ritual Portrayal.* Stanford: Stanford University Press.

Ekman, Paul, and Wallace V. Friesen
1975   *Unmasking the Face.* Englewood Cliffs, N.J.: Prentice-Hall.

Ekman, Paul, Robert Levenson, and Wallace V. Friesen
1983   "Autonomic Nervous System Activity Distinguishes Among Emotions." *Science* 221 (4616): 1208–1210.

Ember, Carol R., and Melvin Ember
1990   *Cultural Anthropology.* 6th ed. Englewood Cliffs, N.J.: Prentice-Hall.

Errington, Shelly
1989   *Meaning and Power in a Southeast Asian Realm.* Princeton: Princeton University Press.

Fairchild, Hoxie Neale
1928   *The Noble Savage: A Study in Romantic Naturalism.* New York: Columbia University Press.

Fiske, John
1989a   *Understanding Popular Culture.* Boston: Unwin Hyman.

1989b   *Reading Popular Culture.* Boston: Unwin Hyman.

Foulcher, Keith
1986   *Social Commitment in Literature and the Arts: The Indonesian "Institute of People's Culture." 1950–1965.* Clayton: Monash University.

Frederick, William H.
1982   "Rhoma Irama and the Dangdut Style: Aspects of Contemporary Indonesian Popular Culture." *Indonesia* 34:102–130.

1985   "Introduction." In *Shackles: A Novel by Armijn Pane.* Athens: Center for International Studies, Ohio University.

1989   *Visions and Heat: The Making of the Indonesian Revolution.* Athens: Ohio University Press.

Gans, Herbert
1988   *Middle American Individualism: The Future of Liberal Democracy.* New York: Free Press.

Geertz, Clifford
1960   *The Religion of Java.* Glencoe: Free Press.

1983   "From the Natives' Point of View: On the Nature of Anthropological Understanding." In *Local Knowledge: Further Essays in Interpretive Anthropology*. New York: Basic Books. (Originally published 1974.)

Geertz, Hildred

1963 "Indonesian Cultures and Communities." In Ruth T. McVey (ed.), *Indonesia*. New Haven: HRAF Press.

1989 *The Javanese Family: A Study of Kinship and Socialization*. Prospect Heights, Ill.: Waveland Press. (Originally published 1961.)

Gertner, Richard (ed.)

1987 *International Motion Picture Almanac*. New York: Quigley.

Gilman, Albert

1963 Introduction to *As You Like It* by William Shakespeare. New York: New American Library.

Goodwin, Charles

1981 *Conversational Organization: Interaction Between Speakers and Hearers*. New York: Academic Press.

Grant, Barry Keith

1986 *Film Genre Reader*. Austin: University of Texas Press.

Hadipurnomo

1988 "What Is Indonesian Cinema?" *Society for Visual Anthropology Newsletter* 4 (1): 15.

Hatley, Barbara

1981 "The Pleasure of the Stage: Images of Love in Javanese Theatre." In Margaret J. Kartomi (ed.), *Five Essays on the Indonesian Arts*. Clayton: Monash University.

1988 "Texts and Contexts: The Roro Mendut Folk Legend on Stage and Screen." In Krishna Sen (ed.), *Histories and Stories: Cinema in New Order Indonesia*. Clayton: Monash University.

n.d. *Ketropak Theatre and the Wayang Tradition*. Working Paper no. 19. Melbourne, Australia: Centre of Southeast Asian Studies, Monash University.

Heider, Karl G.

1975 *Ethnographic Film*. Austin: University of Texas Press.

1990 "Moving Images of the Pacific Islands." *Society For Visual Anthropology Review* 6 (1): 82–84.

1991 *Landscapes of Emotion: Three Maps of Emotion Terms in Indonesia*. New York: Cambridge University Press.

Hellwig, Tineke

1986 "Njai Dasima, een Vrouw uit de literatuur." In C. M. S. Hellwig and S. O. Robson (eds.), *A Man of Indonesian Letters: Essays in Honor of Professor A. Teeuw*. Verhandelingen, Koninklijk Institut voor Taal-, Land-, en Volkenkunde, vol. 121. The Hague: Martinus Nijhoff.

Ihromi, T. O.

1973 "The Relevance of Studying Ethnic Groupings in Indonesia." *Indonesian Quarterly* 2 (1): 24-35.

1980 *Pokok-Pokok Antropologi Budaya.* Jakarta: P. T. Gramedia.

Ismail, Taufiq

1977 "Cerita Angka, FFI 1977." *Tempo* 7 (2), 12 March 1977.

Ismail, Usmar

1956 "The Film Industry." *Atlantic* 197 (6): 141.

1983 *Mengupas Film.* Jakarta: Penerbit Sinar Harapan.

Jackson, Karl D.

1980 *Traditional Authority, Islam, and Rebellion: A Study of Indonesian Political Behavior.* Berkeley: University of California Press.

Jackson, Karl D., and Johannes Moeliono

1973 "Participation in Rebellion: The Dar'ul Islam in West Java." In R. William Liddle (ed.), *Political Participation in Modern Indonesia.* Monograph Series, no. 19. New Haven: Yale University Southeast Asia Studies.

Junus, Umar

1984 *Kaba dan Sistem Social Minangkabau: Suatu Problem Sosiologi Sastra.* Jakarta: PN Balai Pustaka.

Kahin, George McTurnan

1952 *Nationalism and Revolution in Indonesia.* Ithaca: Cornell University Press.

Kaminsky, Stuart M.

1985 *American Film Genres.* 2d ed. Chicago: Nelson-Hall.

Kartomi, Margaret J.

1979 "Minangkabau Musical Culture: The Contemporary Scene and Recent Attempts at Its Modernization." In Gloria Davis (ed.), *What Is Modern Indonesian Culture?* Athens: Center for International Studies, Ohio University.

Karya, Teguh

1983 A speech given in Jakarta, April 12. Published in *Behind the Mosquito Net.* Jakarta: National Film Council.

1988 "In Search of Ways and Means for Making the Film an Instrument of Expression." In Krishna Sen (ed.), *Histories and Stories: Cinema in New Order Indonesia.* Clayton: Monash University.

Kayam, Umar

1981 *Seni, Tradisi, Masyarakat.* Jakarta: Penerbit Sinar Harapan.

Keeler, Ward

1987 *Javanese Shadow Plays, Javanese Selves.* Princeton: Princeton University Press.

Keesing, Roger M.
1989 "Creating the Past: Custom and Identity in the Contemporary Pacific." *The Contemporary Pacific* 1:19–42.

Kipp, Rita Smith
1984 "Terms for Kith and Kin." *American Anthropologist* 86 (4): 905–926.

Koentjaraningrat
1974 "Pembangan Bahasa Indonesia Sebagai Unsur Kebudayaan Nasional." In *Politik Bahasa Nasional, Pra-Seminar.* Jakarta: n.p.

1985 *Javanese Culture.* Singapore: Oxford University Press.

Kottak, Conrad Phillip
1990 *Prime-Time Society: An Anthropological Analysis of Television and Culture.* Belmont, Calif.: Wadsworth.

Kracauer, Siegfried
1947 *From Caligari to Hitler: A Psychological History of the German Film.* Princeton: Princeton University Press.

Kurasawa, Aiko
1987 "Propaganda Media in Java Under the Japanese 1942–1945." *Indonesia* 44:59–116.

Liddle, R. William
1988 *Politics and Culture in Indonesia.* Ann Arbor: Center for Political Studies, Institute for Social Research, University of Michigan.

Lovejoy, Arthur O., and George Boas
1965 *Primitivism and Related Ideas in Antiquity.* New York: Octagon Books. (Originally published 1935.)

Magenda, Burhan D.
1979 "The Press in Jakarta as a Catalyst of Cultural Change." In Gloria Davis (ed.), *What Is Modern Indonesian Culture?* Athens: Center for International Studies, Ohio University.

Marx, Leo
1964 *The Machine in the Garden: Technology and the Pastoral Ideal in America.* New York: Oxford University Press.

Mead, Margaret, and Rhoda Metraux
1953 *The Study of Culture at a Distance.* Chicago: University of Chicago Press.

Mellen, Joan
1976 *The Waves at Genji's Door: Japan Through Its Cinema.* New York: Pantheon.

Misbach Yusa Biran
1973 "Les Vedettes du Cinema Indonesien." *Archipel* 5:165–174.

1982 *Indonesia Cinema: A Glance of History.* Jakarta: National Film Council.

1987 *Snapshots of Indonesian Film History and Non-Theatrical Films in Indonesia.* Jakarta: National Film Council.

Nor, Mohd Anis, M.D.
1986   *Randai Dance of Minangkabau Sumatra with Labanotation Scores.*
        Kuala Lumpur: University of Malaya.

Nourse, Jennifer Jon Williams
1981   "Unity in Diversity: An Anthropological Analysis of Indonesian
        Theater and Film." Master's thesis, Department of Anthropology,
        University of Virginia.

Oetomo, Dede, Daniel Fietkiewicz, and John U. Wolff
1984   *Beginning Indonesian Through Self-Instruction.* Ithaca: Cornell Uni-
        versity, Southeast Asia Program.

Ohnuki-Tierney, Emiko
1990   "The Ambivalent Self of the Contemporary Japanese." *Cultural
        Anthropology* 5 (2): 197–216.

Pane, Armijn
1953   "Produksi Film Tjerita di Indonesia." *Pendidikan Dan Kebudakaan*
        6:1–48.

Peacock, James L.
1987   *Rites of Modernization: Symbolic and Social Aspects of Indonesian
        Proletarian Drama.* 2d ed. Chicago: University of Chicago Press.

Propp, V.
1968   *Morphology of the Folktale.* (English translation.) Austin: Univer-
        sity of Texas Press. (Originally published 1928.)

Provencher, Ronald
1971   *Two Malay Worlds: Interaction in Urban and Rural Settings.* Re-
        search Monograph Series, no. 4. Berkeley, Ca.: Center for South and
        Southeast Asia Studies, University of California.

Rafferty, Ellen
1990   "The New Tradition of Putu Wijaya." *Indonesia* 49:103–116.

Rafferty, Ellen (ed.)
1989   *Putu Wijaya in Performance: A Script and Study of Indonesian The-
        atre.* Monograph 5. Madison: Center for Southeast Asian Studies,
        University of Wisconsin.

Richie, Donald
1988   "Viewing Japanese Film: Some Considerations." In Wimal Dissana-
        yake (ed.), *Cinema and Cultural Identity: Reflections on Films from
        Japan, India, and China.* Lanham, Md.: University Press of Amer-
        ica.

Roeder, O. G.
1969   *The Smiling General: President Soeharto of Indonesia.* Djakarta:
        Gunung Agung.

Roffman, Peter, and Jim Purdy
1981   *The Hollywood Social Problem Film: Madness, Despair, and Politics
        from the Depression to the Fifties.* Bloomington: Indiana University
        Press.

Said, Salim
  1982   *Profil Dunia Film Indonesia.* Jakarta: Grafitipers.

  1987   "The 1987 Indonesian Film Festival: Notes of a Jurist." Unpublished manuscript.

  1989   "Notes on the 1988 Indonesian Film Festival." In *Indonesian Film Festival 1989.* Jakarta: Foreign Relations Division, FFI.

  1990   "Man and Revolutionary Crisis in Indonesian Film." *East-West Film Journal* 4 (2): 111-129.

Sarris, Andrew
  1968   *The American Cinema.* New York: E. P. Dutton.

Schatz, Thomas
  1988   *The Genius of the System: Hollywood Filmmaking in the Studio Era.* New York: Pantheon Books.

Scolnicov, Hanna, and Peter Holland (eds.)
  1989   *The Play Out of Context: Transferring Plays from Culture to Culture.* Cambridge: Cambridge University Press.

Sen, Krishna
  1982   "The Image of Women in Indonesian Films: Some Observations." *Prisma* 24:17-29. (Originally published in the Indonesian language version of *Prisma* in 1981 as "Wajah Wanita Dalam Film Indonesia: Beberapa Catatan.")

  1988   "Filming 'History' Under the New Order." In Krishna Sen (ed.), *Histories and Stories: Cinema in New Order Indonesia.* Clayton: Monash University.

Shaked, Gershon
  1989   "The Play: Gateway to Cultural Dialogue." In Hanna Scolnicov and Peter Holland (eds.), *The Play Out of Context: Transferring Plays from Culture to Culture.* Cambridge: Cambridge University Press.

Shakespeare, William
  1950   *Hamlet: Pangeran Denmark.* Translated by Trisno Sumardjo. Jakarta: Pustaka Jaya.

Siegel, James
  1969   *The Rope of God.* Berkeley: University of California Press.

  1986   *Solo in the New Order: Language and Hierarchy in an Indonesian City.* Princeton: Princeton University Press.

Sinematek Indonesia
  1979   *Apa Siapa: Orang Film Indonesia 1926-1978.* Jakarta: P. T. Metro Pos.

Soemardjono
  1983   "A Glance at the Socio-Cultural Aspect of the Development of Indonesian Film Industry." In *Festival Film Indonesia.* Jakarta: P. T. Karya Sari Offset.

Subagyo Martosubroto
  1979   "Study Tentang Penonton Film." *Berita Buana,* 7 November 1979.

Tanner, Nancy
  1974   "Matrifocality in Indonesia and Africa and Among Black Americans." In Michelle Zimbalist Rosaldo and Louise Lamphere (eds.), *Women, Culture, and Society.* Stanford: Stanford University Press.

Taylor, Jean Gelman
  1976   "Raden Adjeng Kartini." *Signs* 1 (3): 639–661.

  1989   "Kartini in Her Historical Context." *Bijdragen* tot de Taal-, Land-, en Volkenkunde 145 (2/3): 295–307.

Thompson, Stith
  1977   *The Folktale.* Berkeley: University of California Press. (Originally published 1946.)

Weakland, John
  1966a   "Themes in Chinese Communist Films." *American Anthropologist* 68 (2): 477–484 (special issue).

  1966b   *Chinese Political and Cultural Themes: A Study of Chinese Communist Films.* China Lake, Calif.: U.S. Naval Ordnance Test Station.

  1971   "Real and Reel Life in Hong Kong—Film Studies of Cultural Adaptation?" *Journal of Asian and African Studies* 1 (3–4): 238–242.

  1972   "Conflicts Between Love and Family Relationships in Chinese Films." *Journal of Popular Film* 1:290–298.

Wellenkamp, Jane C.
  1988   "Order and Disorder in Toraja Thought and Ritual." *Ethnology* 27 (3): 311–326.

White, Hayden
  1972   "The Forms of Wildness: Archaeology of an Idea." In Edward Dudley and Maximillian E. Novak (eds.), *The Wild Man Within.* Pittsburgh: University of Pittsburgh Press.

Wolfenstein, Martha, and Nathan Leites
  1950   *Movies: A Psychological Study.* Glencoe, Ill.: Free Press.

Wright, Will
  1975   *Sixguns and Society: A Structural Study of the Western.* Berkeley: University of California Press.

Yampolsky, Philip
  1989   *"Hati Yang Luka,* An Indonesian Hit." *Indonesia* 47:1–17.

INDEX

Advertisements, 11, 12, 24, 25, 89–92 (photos 1–4); for comedy films, 25; regional variations in, 12; women in, 116–118

AIB, 9

Akibat Kanker Payudara, 54, 63

Alien: in tale type, 46–52

Allan, Jeremy, 99

Anderson, Benedict, 33, 34, 36, 74

Anderson, Charles, 103, 105

Anthropological approaches to cinema, 3–6

Anwar, Khaidir, 139

Ardan, S. M., 11, 15

Arie Hanggara, 45, 54

As You Like It, 56, 57

Audiences, 11, 12, 20–22, 45, 88; age of, 21; and reaction to Dani films, 115; regional variations in, 21; versus television, 21, 22

Auteur films, 5, 6, 30, 42, 55, 87; cultural roots of, 131, 132

Ayahku, 121

Ayu Dan Ayu, 54, 55, 118, 119

Bachtiar, Harsya, 10, 74

Badai Pasti Berlalu, 54, 63

"Banana peel" signs. *See* Conventions, narrative

Bateson, Gregory, 114

Beauty and the Beast, 49, 50

Becker, A. L., 52, 88

Becker, Judith, 5

Beeman, William, 4

Benedict, Ruth, 4, 28

Bernheimer, Richard, 110, 115

Blue Lagoon, The, 45, 112–115, 126–128

Boas, George, 110

Bordwell, David, 139

Brahmana Manggala, 89 (Photo 1)

Brandon, James, 37

Bruner, Edward M., 10, 11

Buah Hati Mama, 45, 53, 54

Buaya Putih, 44, 54, 59, 61, 62, 67

Budak Nafsu, 42, 47

Bukan Sandiwara, 54

Caldarola, Victor, 4

Canby, Vincent, 123

Carok, 45, 68, 86

Censorship, 22, 23, 66

Chinese: assimilation of, 133, 134; as characters in films, 64, 73, 80, 81, 106, 107, 133–138; and role in film industry, 15, 16; stereotyping of, 133; and tension, 73

Cintaku Di Kampus Biru, 8, 67, 68, 86

Citra awards, 6, 23–24, 42; compared with Oscars, 23

Clowns, 85

Comedy: advertisements for, 25; as genre, 45; in Horror films, 44, 67; about "primitive" peoples, 113; zooming lens in, 70

Conventions, narrative: alcohol, 60, 75; "banana peel" signs, 62–64; bathing in pool, 63; betel chewing, 61, 76; breaking glass, 63, 138; ethnic ceremonies, 59; hospital breezeway setting, 59, 92 (Photo 5); loose hair, 61, 93 (Photo 6); landscapes, 58, 59; palm-to-palm contact, 67, 68; paralinguistic sigh, 64; scissors, 62, 63; of sexuality, 66–69; stocks, 62, 93 (Photo 6); tobacco, 61; vomiting, 59, 60; zooming lens, 70. *See also* Sexuality

Conversion, sudden, 83

Culture, national Indonesian, 3, 10–13, 26–38, 76, 133–140; group oriented, 29–36, 125, 126, 128–132, 136; and concern with order and disorder, 25, 28–30, 34–38, 51–53, 56, 57, 60, 62, 76, 136, 137

Culture, theory of, 12, 28, 29, 34; changing, 13

Danandjaja, James, 40, 46

Dani, reactions to films about, 115

Darah Dan Do'a, 17, 102–106, 128–132

Desa Di Kaki Bukit, 60, 61, 73, 81–86, 95 (Photo 9) 133, 136

Dia Sang Penakluk, 112

Di Balik Kelambu, 54

Djajakusuma, 14, 17

Djarot, Eros, 27, 42
Doea Tanda Mata, 4, 54, 55, 70, 99, 100, 131, 132
Doherty, Thomas, 21
Drake, Christine, 21, 22
Dundes, Alan, 46

Edwards, Walter, 31
Ekman, Paul, 65
Eman Djam Di Jogya, 101
Ember, Carol R., 33
Ember, Melvin, 33
Emotion: the anger face, 64, 65, 94 (photos 7, 8); confusion as, 38, 61; as inner state versus interaction, 32–34; research on, 7–9, 11, 27, 29, 32, 38, 64
Errington, Shelly, 37
European influence in Indonesian cinema, 12, 15, 16, 18, 129, 130
Evil: in Western films, 51; versus disorder, 29. *See also* Culture, national Indonesian

False accusation: in Sentimental plots, 52–55
Fairchild, Hoxie Neale, 110
Feminism, 116–121
Fietkiewicz, Daniel, 33
Film Festival Indonesian, 21, 23, 24. *See also* Citra awards
Film theories, 2, 3: as agent of change, 16, 17–25, 134; as reflection of culture, 2, 3, 26–38
Fiske, John, 88
Flaherty, Robert, 110
Folk ethnography. *See* Other, The
Folklore in film, 40, 44, 49; and tale type approach, 46–67
Foulcher, Keith, 17
Frederick, William H., 16, 45, 74, 137
Friesen, Wallace V., 65

Galau Remaja Di SMA, 60
Gans, Herbert, 31
Geertz, Clifford, 30, 36
Geertz, Hildred, 10, 119
Genre, 5, 6, 30, 39–46, 87, 118; Anak-Anak, Kid Films, 45; Expedition, 45; Horror, 43, 44; Komedi, 45; Kompeni, 40–42, 47; Japanese Period, 42, 47, 49, 50; Legend, 40, 46; Musicals, 45; Science Fiction, absence of, 108; Sentimental, 43, 52–55, 120, 133; Struggle for Independence, 42, 43, 99–107; versus auteur approach, 5, 6
Gertner, Richard, 19, 20
Gilman, Albert, 57
Goodwin, Charles, 3
Grand Illusion, 130
Grant, Barry Keith, 5, 45, 46

Hadipurnomo, 10
Hamlet, 32, 33
Hatley, Barbara, 18, 37
Hellwig, Tineke, 15
History, revisions of Indonesian, 99–107
History of Indonesian cinema, 15–18, 138
Holland, Peter, 122
Humor. *See* Comedy
Hunchback of Notre Dame, The, 48, 50

Ibunda, 115, 121
Ihromi, T. O., 10, 33
Individual versus group. *See* Culture, national Indonesian
Indonesian culture change, theory of, 74
Intan Perawan Kubu, 112
Ismail, Nawi, 129
Ismail, Taufiq, 27
Ismail, Usmar, 12, 14, 15, 17, 101, 103, 129–131

Jackson, Karl D., 102
Jaka Gledek, 41
Jaka Sembung, 41
Japanese: occupation by, 16, 17; influence on films, 16
Johanna, 47, 50
Jungle Princess, The, 15

Kaba (epic poems): influence on Sentimental genre, 43
Kadarwati, 42, 47, 66
Kahin, George McTurnan, 16, 101, 102, 104
Kali Seraya, 137
Kaminsky, Stuart M., 5
Kamp Tawanan Wanita, 42, 47
Kamus Cinta Sang Primadona, 90 (Photo 2)
Kartini figure, 75, 76, 120, 121; in *Cintaku Di Kampus Biru,* 87; in *Desa Di Kaki Bukit,* 83, 84; in *Salah Asuhan,* 80
Kartomi, Margaret, 10

Karya, Teguh, 6, 9, 14-16, 55, 100, 115, 131
Keeler, Ward, 18, 37, 71, 88
Keesing, Roger, 109
Keluarga Markum, 91 (Photo 3)
Kerinduan, 54
King Kong, 48, 50, 51, 111; and absent plot model, 49
King Lear, 34, 35, 123
Kipp, Rita, 34
Koentjaraningrat, 10
Kottak, Conrad, 4, 6
Kracauer, Siegfried, 4, 71
Kupa Kupa Putih, 45
Kurasawa, Aiko, 16

Language, Indonesian: in films, 16, 26, 27, 139
Leach, Sir Edmund, 9
Lebak Membara, 42, 47
Leites, Nathan, 4, 9, 48, 71, 123-126
LEKRA, 17
LESBUMI, 17
Levenson, Robert, 65
Lewat Djam Malam, 130
Liddle, R. William, 10
Loetoeng Kasaroeng (Lutung Kasarung), 15, 40, 46, 47, 50, 114
Loro Jonggrang, 40
Lovejoy, Arthur O., 110
Ludruk (theater), 2, 3, 21, 37, 71, 72, 74; *Pak Sakerah* as, 41, 42; clowns in, 85

McGlynn, John, 100
Magenda, Burhan D., 10
Magic powers. *See* Supernatural
Malam Satu Suro, 44
Marriage, arranged, 31
Marx, Leo, 111
Max Havelaar, 22
Mead, Margaret, 4
Melatie Van Java, 15
Mellen, Joan, 71
Melodrama. *See* Genre: Sentimental
Mereka Kembali, 60, 61, 103-107, 128-133
Methodology, 9
Metraux, Rhoda, 4
Misbach Yusa Biran, 9, 15
Moana, 110, 111
Moeliono, Johannes, 102
Moonstruck, 124

National Indonesian culture. *See* Culture, national Indonesian
Nightmare on Elm Street, 44
Nila Digaun Putih, 54
Njai Dasima, 15, 133. See also *Samiun Dan Dasima*
Noer, Arifin C., 101
Nor, Mohd Anis, 18
November 1828, 42

Oetomo, Dede, 33
Ohnuki-Tierney, Emiko, 4
Order and disorder: and drunkenness, 60; and loose hair, 61, 137; as result of mixed schooling, 81; and shaven head, 137; and stocks, 62, 93 (Photo 6); in wayang, 52; and zooming camera, 25
Other, The, 108-115; as Noble Savage, 110; as Ignoble Savage, 110, 111; as alien, 46-52; in *Blue Lagoon/Pengantin Pantai Biru,* 127, 128

Pacar Ketinggalan Kereta, 9, 14
Pagar Kawat Berduri, 130
Pak Sakerah, 41
Pane, Armijn, 15
Paralinguistic sigh, 64
Pareh, 15
Peacock, James L., 2, 3, 18, 21, 37, 41, 74, 85; and theater as agent of change, 71-72
Pedjuang, 130
Pengantin Pantai Biru, 45, 112-115, 126-128
Perempuan Dalam Pasungan, 54, 61, 62, 69, 93 (Photo 6)
Ponirah Terpandana, 45
Pramoedya Ananta Toer, 22
Primitive tribes, 112. *See also* Other, The
Production, 9; yearly figures for, 16, 18, 19 (Table 1), 20; rates compared, 20
Propp, V., 46
Provencher, Ronald, 137
Punishment: absence of, 52, 54, 137, 138; as key to recognizing pattern, 38
Purdy, Jim, 134
Putri Giok, 45, 54, 73, 133-138

Rafferty, Ellen, 18, 81
Raja Copet, 94 (photos 7, 8), 133
Rambo, 45, 87
Ran, 35, 40

Ratu Pantai Selatan, 40
Rebel Without a Cause, 33
Regional culture, film representations of, 11
Religon, 27, 104; and art, 69; Islamic, 135; in Sentimental genre films, 43; used iconically, 135
Remakes. *See* Translations/transformations
Richie, Donald, 139
Rocky, 45, 87
Roeder, O. G., 101
Roffman, Peter, 134
Romeo and Juliet, 31, 124
Roro Mendut, 40

Said, Salim, 14–17, 27, 43, 105, 138
Salah Asuhan, 60, 68, 76–81, 86, 95 (Photo 10), 98 (Photo 14), 133
Samiun Dan Dasima, 60, 64, 69. See also *Njai Dasima*
Sani, Asrul, 14, 17, 18, 81, 82, 86, 130, 131
Sarangan Fajar, 101
Sarris, Andrew, 5
Saur Sepuh, 40
Schatz, Thomas, 5
Scolnicov, Hanna, 122
Sen, Krishna, 15, 22–24, 116, 118, 138
Serpihan Mutiara Retak, 54
Sexuality, 23, 24, 27, 66–69; absent in Sentimental genre, 43; in advertisements, 96–97 (photos 11, 12), 117; in *Blue Lagoon,* 127, 128; body display in, 63, 69, 75; conventions of, 63; as disorder, 62; in Horror genre, 44; in Japanese Period genre, 42; as Modern-Western attribute, 84; palm-to-palm handholding as, 67, 68, 95 (photos 9, 10), 117, 138; red clothing as sign of, 69. *See also* Conventions, narrative
Si Doel Anak Betawi, 11, 45, 61, 63, 69
Siegel, James, 18, 71, 119
Siregar, Ashadi, 8, 87
Si Unyil, 45

Social problem films, 134, 138
Subagyo, Martosubroto, 21
Suicide, 137
Supernatural powers: in Horror genre, 43, 44; in Kompeni genre, 41; in Legend genre, 40; in Sentimental genre, absence of, 43
Syumandjaya, 131

Tale types: Female Captive Loved by Alien Male Captor, 46–52; Family Separation and Reunion, 52–57
Tampopo, 4
Tan's Film, 15, 17
Tanner, Nancy, 119
Taylor, Jean Gelman, 75
Tempest, The, 111
Terang Boelan, 15, 16
Theater genres, other, 18
Thompson, Stith, 46
Tiga Dara, 14
Tirai Malam Pengantin, 54
Tjut Nya Dien, 22, 27, 42, 77, 121
Translations/transformations, 122, 123: in advertising, 24; of American films, 45, 126–128; of *Blue Lagoon,* 126–128; of *Cousins,* 124–126; of emotion words, 32–34; of Indonesian films, 128–132; of *King Lear* into Japanese, 34, 35; of *Pak Sakerah* in luruk and film, 41, 42
Typee, 111

Walkabout, 48–51
Wayang, 18, 21, 25, 36–38, 40, 52, 71, 88, 114
Weakland, John, 4
Wellenkamp, Jane, 37
West Side Story, 124
Wijaya, Putu, 9
Wolfenstein, Martha, 4, 9, 48, 71, 123–126
Wolff, John U., 33
Women: in ethnographies, 119, 120; images of, 116–121
Wong Brothers, 15–17
Wright, Will, 3, 6, 46